Off-Road Disciplines

Off-Road Disciplines

Spiritual Adventures of Missional Leaders

Earl Creps

Foreword by Dan Kimball

A LEADERSHIP ❋ NETWORK PUBLICATION

JOSSEY-BASS
A Wiley Imprint
www.josseybass.com

Published by Jossey-Bass
A Wiley Imprint
989 Market Street, San Francisco, CA 94103–1741   www.josseybass.com

Jossey-Bass books and products are available through most bookstores. To contact Jossey-Bass directly call our Customer Care Department within the U.S. at 800-956-7739, outside the U.S. at 317-572-3986, or fax 317-572-4002.

Jossey-Bass also publishes its books in a variety of electronic formats. Some content that appears in print may not be available in electronic books.

All Scripture quotations, unless otherwise indicated, are taken from the HOLY BIBLE, NEW INTERNATIONAL VERSION®. NIV®. Copyright © 1973, 1978, 1984 by International Bible Society. Used by permission of Zondervan. All rights reserved.

Excerpt from "Evangelizing Folk Religionists," by Gailyn Van Rheenen. March 12, 2002, e-mail newsletter (missiological-reflections@lists.acu.edu). Copyright 2003 by Gailyn Van Rheenen. Reprinted with permission from Gailyn Van Rheenen.

Excerpt from "An Interview with U2's Bono," by Peter Mansbridge. June 28, 2002, http://www.atu2.com/news/article.src?ID=2364. Copyright CBC, 2002. All rights reserved. Reprinted with permission from the CBC.

Excerpt from "A Theology to Die For," by Timothy George. February 9, 1998, http://www.ctlibrary.com/ct/1998/february9/8t2049.html. Reprinted with permission from Timothy George.

Library of Congress Cataloging-in-Publication Data

Creps, Earl G.
    Off-road disciplines: spiritual adventures of missional leaders / Earl Creps; foreword by Dan Kimball.
       p. cm.
    Includes bibliographical references.
    ISBN-13: 978-0-7879-8520-2 (cloth)
    ISBN-10: 0-7879-8520-1 (cloth)
    1. Christian leadership. 2. Leadership, Religious aspects—Christianity. I. Title.
    BV652.1.C735 2006
    253—dc22   2006020384

Printed in the United States of America
FIRST EDITION
HB Printing   10 9 8 7 6 5 4 3 2 1

Leadership Network Titles

The Blogging Church: Sharing the Story of Your Church Through Blogs, by Brian Bailey with Terry Storch

Leading from the Second Chair: Serving Your Church, Fulfilling Your Role, and Realizing Your Dreams, by Mike Bonem and Roger Patterson

The Way of Jesus: A Journey of Freedom for Pilgrims and Wanderers, by Jonathan S. Campbell with Jennifer Campbell

Leading the Team-Based Church: How Pastors and Church Staffs Can Grow Together into a Powerful Fellowship of Leaders, by George Cladis

Organic Church: Growing Faith Where Life Happens, by Neil Cole

Off-Road Disciplines: Spiritual Adventures of Missional Leaders, by Earl Creps

Leading Congregational Change Workbook, by James H. Furr, Mike Bonem, and Jim Herrington

Leading Congregational Change: A Practical Guide for the Transformational Journey, by Jim Herrington, Mike Bonem, and James H. Furr

The Leader's Journey: Accepting the Call to Personal and Congregational Transformation, by Jim Herrington, Robert Creech, and Trisha Taylor

Culture Shift: Transforming Your Church from the Inside Out, by Robert Lewis and Wayne Cordeiro, with Warren Bird

A New Kind of Christian: A Tale of Two Friends on a Spiritual Journey, by Brian D. McLaren

The Story We Find Ourselves In: Further Adventures of a New Kind of Christian, by Brian D. McLaren

Practicing Greatness: 7 Disciplines of Extraordinary Spiritual Leaders, by Reggie McNeal

The Present Future: Six Tough Questions for the Church, by Reggie McNeal

A Work of Heart: Understanding How God Shapes Spiritual Leaders, by Reggie McNeal

The Millennium Matrix: Reclaiming the Past, Reframing the Future of the Church, by M. Rex Miller

Shaped by God's Heart: The Passion and Practices of Missional Churches, by Milfred Minatrea

The Ascent of a Leader: How Ordinary Relationships Develop Extraordinary Character and Influence, by Bill Thrall, Bruce McNicol, and Ken McElrath

The Missional Leader: Equipping Your Church to Reach a Changing World, by Alan J. Roxburgh and Fred Romanuk

The Elephant in the Boardroom: Speaking the Unspoken About Pastoral Transitions, by Carolyn Weese and J. Russell Crabtree

Contents

About Leadership Network

Since 1984, Leadership Network has fostered church innovation and growth by diligently pursuing its far-reaching mission statement: to identify, connect, and help high-capacity Christian leaders multiply their impact.

Although Leadership Network's techniques adapt and change as the church faces new opportunities and challenges, the organization's work follows a consistent and proven pattern: Leadership Network brings together entrepreneurial leaders who are focused on similar ministry initiatives. The ensuing collaboration—often across denominational lines—creates a strong base from which individual leaders can better analyze and refine their own strategies. Peer-to-peer interaction, dialogue, and sharing inevitably accelerate participants' innovation and ideas. Leadership Network further enhances this process through developing and distributing highly targeted ministry tools and resources, including audio and video programs, special reports, e-publications, and online downloads.

With Leadership Network's assistance, today's Christian leaders are energized, equipped, inspired, and better able to multiply their own dynamic Kingdom-building initiatives.

Launched in 1996 in conjunction with Jossey-Bass (a Wiley imprint), Leadership Network publications present thoroughly researched and innovative concepts from leading thinkers, practitioners, and pioneering churches. The series collectively draws from a range of disciplines, with individual titles offering perspective on one or more of five primary areas:

1. Enabling effective leadership
2. Encouraging life-changing service
3. Building authentic community
4. Creating Kingdom-centered impact
5. Engaging cultural and demographic realities

For additional information on the mission or activities of Leadership Network, please contact:

Leadership Network
www.leadnet.org
(800) 765-5323
client.care@leadnet.org

Foreword

For as long as the current "Emerging Church" discussion has been going on, the name Earl Creps keeps coming up. Earl is very much a scholar, and he has his Ph.D. and is a professor at the Assemblies of God Theological Seminary (AGTS). But in addition to his academic credentials and experience in that world, Earl is no stranger to the reality of being a leader in the local church. He has served as a pastor three times and knows well the daily struggles and ups and downs of the real world beyond seminary. So with Earl you get an alloy of academic skills and knowledge with a background in actual pastoral ministry—a rare combination.

It doesn't end there. Earl has been listening, dialoguing, traveling, visiting, and studying churches and leadership the whole time. I have often gone to his Website (http://www.earlcreps.com/) and blog (http://www.xanga.com/Coffeedrinkinfool) to glean from his vast exposure to what the Spirit of God is doing within the Church in our emerging culture. He has incredibly broad experience as a scout who sees patterns in churches and leadership. As a well-traveled explorer of the Church over many years, Earl offers more than description of the latest cool topics in leadership; we see instead what the Spirit of God is doing that is lasting and bearing fruit, that transcends any methodology or trend in church leadership. This broader and more creative view is what we all need to seek.

In your hands you have a book that has been simmering and brewing over all these years of Earl's scouting and learning. You hold something that is rich, cured, and aged to sink into your mind and heart in a way that couldn't happen without breadth of experience behind it. This isn't a book about a quick fix to break an attendance barrier, or bringing in new music or a new design for a worship gathering. It isn't about how to give better sermons. Earl writes about the most important thing he has discovered in all his exploring of the Church: the life of the missional leader and its effect on a missional organization.

Leadership is critical. I believe what we need in the Church today is not just leaders but *missional* leaders. Not every church rises to Jesus' charge to reach out to the world. Not all church leaders respond to such a mission. Many of them fall into the trap of striving only for bigger and better programs or music, or whatever, for the already saved. Being a missional leader is entirely different. We need to prepare for the mission by developing patterns and disciplines in our lives and ministry that the Spirit of God can use to sustain us while we serve Jesus on His mission. This book is a readable and understandable exploration of the patterns of discipline that missional leaders need in their lives. More than theory or nice thoughts, this book is written from being in the depths of missional leadership and from observing and watching what the Spirit of God is doing in churches and leaders in many places, over many years.

I am excited about the impact this book will definitely have in changing leaders' lives. It is also written for the people Jesus loves and cares about who will follow and be changed by leaders practicing the disciplines Earl speaks of. My prayer for this book is that God may use it missionally—and as I type these words I pray for those who may never even read it themselves but instead be influenced by the lives of those who do.

Dan Kimball, author, *The Emerging Church*
www.vintagefaith.com

Introduction

Kevin left his job as an environmental consultant to become an entrepreneur. Sensing a once-in-a-lifetime opportunity at hand, he set up the coffee shop he had always wanted to own and operate with his family, in a suburb on the south end of our city. A few months into his venture and wanting his business somehow to help people connect with God, Kevin contacted local churches about the possibility of partnering with them to touch the city. Because we had worked together in a local church, Kevin knew of my interest in this subject and e-mailed me about the response of the congregational leaders.

Of course, there are the obvious differences in superficial stuff: style, denominational background, and so on. But I found the difference in definition of and approach to their mission even more interesting. I recall some who are passionate about making ways for the culture to come to Christ, while others were, let's say, less passionate; still others just didn't see much benefit in talking about it with me. Some of these meetings have been electric, while others have seemed pretty empty. Some meetings have been entirely about how we could work together, while regarding others people either didn't respond or were coldly polite. The responses did not follow variables of style or labels.

Kevin's informal sampling of church cultures revealed, in just a few weeks, two key dynamics that scholars of the Church have labored for years to discover: (1) leaders with a missional heart find a way, no matter how unconventional, to connect to culture; and

(2) this heart is present (and absent) in every conceivable model of ministry.

Missional leaders see the world through the eyes of Jesus and see Jesus in the world. They assume the role of helping the body of Christ understand itself and make of it much more than a missionary sending agency, as if the "mission field" existed only somewhere else to be reached by someone else. Rather, these leaders cannot conceive of the Church apart from living the mission of God to touch the world with redeeming love in Christ. "The classical doctrine of the *missio Dei*," explains missiologist David Bosch, "as God the Father sending the Son, and God the Father and the Son sending the Spirit, [is] expanded to include yet another 'movement': Father, Son, and Holy Spirit sending the church into the world."[1] For missional leaders, then, mission does not refer to a framed paragraph hanging on the wall in the lobby and printed on all the staff business cards; it refers instead to the Church's very reason for being. To remove it or replace does not just make the Church less effective; it changes the Church into something else, something that does not resemble the New Testament account of our identity as a sent people.

In practical terms, it is not difficult to demonstrate the vital role that mission plays in the vibrancy of Christian ministry. Studies of denominations and surveys of individual Christians find a leader's vision to reach a community indispensable to the growth and health of the Church, regardless of the specific philosophy of ministry involved.[2] But references to academic scholarship are hardly necessary. Any church member on any Sunday can tell you that either mission lives in the heart of leaders or it does not live at all. So, how is such a heart developed?

Off-Road Disciplines

This book argues that missional leadership derives not from methods or strategies but from the work of the Holy Spirit to rearrange one's interior life. This work is accomplished by rigorous application of what I call *spiritual disciplines*. You will find that my list of disciplines bears little resemblance to most of the practices traditionally thought of in this way. Although Richard Foster's classic tally in *Celebration of Discipline* includes what he calls "Outward" and "Corporate" disciplines, the average leader that I know mainly thinks of spiritual disciplines in terms of prayer and Bible reading.[3] These two pillars of spiritual growth entail several dilemmas:

- *Scarcity*: despite their benefits, they are not practiced enough.
- *Practicality*: these two disciplines tend to operate in isolation from real life, serving as the "national anthem" before the ball game that starts whenever we go to work.
- *Performance*: they cannot be correlated to ministry "success" in any consistent way; in other words, unspiritual people accomplish a lot while more spiritual people labor in obscurity.
- *Character*: to speak for myself, I've met too many bad people who pray and read their Bibles rigorously and are unchanged by their efforts.
- *Mission*: churches are filled with people who are committed to prayer and Scripture but either have no concern for mission or actively resist the changes that it requires.

Most of these dilemmas spring from the way prayer and Scripture study are isolated from the rest of the Christian life. As Foster contends, "the Disciplines are best exercised in the midst of our normal daily activities. If they are to have any transforming effect, the effect must be found in the ordinary junctures of human life."[4] In other words, our practice of the disciplines tends to be undisciplined.

However, if we do indeed meet God at the sidewalk level, then perhaps a missional heart can be formed in the same way by practicing what I call "off-road" disciplines, ones that seldom appear in more formal catalogues. In other words, the on-road practices of prayer and Bible reading should be supplemented by the other kinds of encounter with God that occur unexpectedly—complete with the bumps and bruises that are part of any other form of off-road experience. I contend here that an experience is a spiritual discipline if it has the *potential* to form God's heart in me, and if it *functions* as one because I embrace it as such. So, for example, death (Chapter One) represents a spiritual discipline when the collapse of my ministry paradigms creates the opportunity to crucify my longing to be the center of everything. In the end, the off-road disciplines, both personal and organizational serve to *decenter* me and my ideas by freeing up the place where Christ rightfully belongs in my life, my leadership, and my organization. As John the Baptist described it, "He must become greater; I must become less."[5]

This book is organized into two main sections, one personal and one organizational. Part One depicts six disciplines that shape the interior life of missional leaders as individuals, while Part Two offers the same number for the organizations we lead. In truth, this division was never part of the plan for the book. I only realized after the fact that the chapters fell into this alignment, perhaps subconsciously reflecting my belief that organizations are fundamentally spiritual, possessing an *interior life* of their own and requiring spiritual disciplines every bit as much as individual people do. I understand Christian leadership as spiritual direction for the interior life of organizations. On both levels, the off-road disciplines serve the function of making space in our lives so that Jesus assumes the central position within us and the Spirit conforms us to the mission. The alternative is to reduce mission to evangelism, evangelism to a program, a program to a strategy, and strategy to a technology we can control. Mission is everything Jesus came to do; it calls us to co-labor in the things we cannot control. A missional leader, then, lives under the often painful influence of these disciplines for the sake of forming the church into a sent people. I conclude that living a missional life of any kind is quite difficult, given the punishing experiences that seem to be necessary to maintain it. I want, with every fiber of my being, to be the center, and my natural longing for the central position does not die easily. It takes a cross.

Deconstructing Myself

Having spent years in relationship with natives to postmodernity (one element of our cultural "perfect storm"), I have learned the value of deconstructing myself, of letting others know that I am aware that my point of view is just that: a view from a point. They are already aware of these dynamics, but it is important that they realize that I am aware of them as well. So even though this book features some quotes and notes, these materials are not really its sources. These are the wellsprings of my work:

- My *life:* I am a middle-class, Anglo, male baby boomer who grew up a Lutheran pastor's son, joining the Assemblies of God as a refugee from the 1970s Charismatic renewal in my denomination of origin.
- My *beliefs:* I am almost painfully orthodox doctrinally, but with a Pentecostal identity bundled with a Mainliner's open-mindedness.
- My *research:* I have spent several years traveling North America on behalf of my seminary, interviewing younger leaders in particular, and anyone who is doing anything different in general. I quote them using pseudonyms (sometimes), not at their request but out of respect for the risks some of them took to talk to me.
- My *experience:* I have pastored three congregations, all Assemblies of God: one boomer, one builder, and one gen X.
- My *sins:* much of this book is informed by my own shortcomings. Some friends are uncomfortable with this aspect of my writing, but I feel that the only way to rob these issues of power is to tell their stories and convert them to learnings.
- My *friends:* you will sense at once that this book is really the story of the people I have met in my travels who have been kind enough to share their lives with me. I owe them everything, especially the young ones such as Mark and Kevin, who made me a guest in their world. I hope I have been good company. Whenever I refer to an interview, I am quoting their remarks verbatim from

transcripts. However, when I just bracket their comments with quotation marks, I am reconstructing their words from memory, probably making our exchanges a little better than they actually were.

• *My love:* In a small seminar several years ago, someone asked me how I had been influenced by all my field work. The answer: "I love the Church more." In the end, this book is born out of that love, and out of the conviction that we must love the Church more than our interpretation of it.

Taken collectively, these sources have conspired to produce both my list of off-road disciplines and my belief that they hold one key to forming leaders who will measure success by how effectively they live out Jesus' charge: "As the Father has sent me, I am sending you."[6] These leaders will be glad to work with Kevin in his coffee house.

Off-Road Disciplines

For Janet

Part One

Personal Disciplines

Chapter One

Death

The Discipline of Personal Transformation

"If what you're saying about emerging culture is true, how should I change my church?"

A question like this seems almost inevitable when I speak to groups of ministers. A few seconds of silence usually follow as the others in the room dial in their full attention to hear my response. In their minds, they have paid to come to the conference for this moment, for my "deliverable." The second almost-inevitable question is, "What's working really well in the innovative churches you have visited?" The questioner here determines to elicit a set of best practices that could be imported into her or his ministry.

The commonsense pragmatism driving these questions elevates ministry *technique* as the starting point for thinking about mission. "How should we do our worship services?" the anxious, balding pastor asks me. Softly, I reply, "You may be asking the wrong question first." My answer, hopefully, suggests a more difficult but more primary question: *How can I be changed so that others will find me worth following in mission?* The way to develop a missional ministry, then, is to be transformed into a missional person, "so that everyone may see your progress."[1] In the end, my best practice must be me.

The priority of the interior life defies conventional attempts at documentation. But I have seen it and lived it. In fact, virtually every influential leader I know in the Emerging Church points to a crisis of personal transformation as a major source of ministry to postmoderns. This chapter relates some of my own journey from teenage convert through the wilderness of professional ministry, and back out to missionary-in-training. A pattern emerges in the

3

narratives that follow: new life often emerges from some kind of death. The kind of spiritual renovation that forms a missionary's heart defies every attempt at reduction to a formula, or franchising as a "model." But there is a common confession, along with Paul: "I have been crucified with Christ, and I no longer live, but Christ lives in me."[2]

I call these small "crucifixions" *paradigm crashes*. A paradigm expresses my basic orientation toward how the ministry works; it is my "operating system" of unspoken premises that runs in the background unattended. Most of us simply assume our paradigms, just as we assume our breathing. A crash happens when pain makes the frailty of those assumptions impossible to ignore, just as an asthma attack makes breathing the most important thing in life for a few minutes. Sometimes violent, sometimes gradual, paradigm crashes create an opportunity for God to take me off road, awakening me to mission by crucifying aspects of my culture, leadership, and spirituality that, unbeknownst to me, need to die.

Nuclear War and Other Problems: The Cultural Paradigm

I learned early in life that the world is a very serious place. My parents seemed more worried than normal, not surprising given the news reports about the Soviets having positioned nuclear missiles in Cuba for a sneak attack on the United States. Later I would learn to call this episode the "Cuban Missile Crisis"—just one of many crises in my Cold War childhood. In school, we pored over creased copies of *Life* magazine searching the photographs and drawings for clues that might explain why the end of the world was at hand. Living in Pittsburgh, the home of the American steel industry at the time, we knew that somewhere on a wall in the Kremlin there hung a map with a red bull's-eye printed on our zip code.

Of course, a sixth grader doesn't really possess the coping skills for an apocalypse, so our elementary school tried to ease the stress of my nuclear youth with a strategy something like a nuclear fire drill. Under our teacher's direction, we filed out of our home room into the long linoleum corridor. Our defensive doctrine required the student body to be formed into a human phalanx by lining up half a dozen twelve-year-olds so close to the wall that their foreheads touched the cool beige tile. The rest of us each put a forearm across the shoulders of one of these anchor students, and then rested our forehead on it. This process continued until every student's forehead-on-forearm combination connected to the shoulder blades of another student to form a rough square about five sixth graders on a side.

Oliver, Jeff, Wendy, and the others practiced the atomic phalanx with me over and over, until forming a bomb shelter made of flesh required little effort. To add emphasis to our training, we froze for a moment in the forehead-on-forearm position, as if bowing our heads together in a moment of mass prayer, last rites for the atomic age. The idea behind the phalanx seemed simple: if enough sixth graders assembled, a few of us in the middle of the formation might survive the blast and heat produced by the first shower of ICBMs. After that, I guess we were all on our own.

Eventually, our bomb-shelter-made-of-skin exercise started to get to me. Even as a twelve-year-old, I knew too much—too much *Life* magazine. Everything ended after a full-scale nuclear exchange. It was flash—agony—darkness. In fact, the temporary survivors inherited the worst of it, so why rehearse fantasy defensive scenarios? If the Nike missiles and Delta fighters that guarded the skies over our city missed even one inbound Soviet weapon, our pitiful student formations only rearranged the casualties.

The truth arrived, like a sneak attack, several years later: somewhere, someone with authority believed that, if the worst happened, sixth graders should at least be melted into the linoleum in perfectly straight lines. Proper "deportment," as our teachers called good conduct in those days, demanded compliance to the very end.

Like Dorothy and her friends in the *Wizard of Oz*, my glimpse of the man behind the curtain changed everything. The people I trusted (parents, teachers, presidents) asked us to face Armageddon wearing armor with only two layers, polyester and skin, while they hid like Dr. Strangelove in bunkers beneath mountain ranges. From their hideouts, in a fit of rage or a moment of miscalculation, they might even end the world I counted on them to maintain. The phalanx exercises served to keep us all distracted and deceived, preempting any questioning of their motives or their right to lead. The madness of it all began my personal postmodern turn, otherwise known as the sixties.

Crucified Culture

The trauma of the human bomb shelter concealed a gift. The society I knew as the ground of all being looked different to me now, filled with contradictions, flaws, and corruptions. Blind devotion to the values of conservative, modern, Anglo suburbia began to feel like dedication to the idea of a flat earth. Ironically, Christians question me at times about the danger of the Church being corrupted by twenty-first-century culture, fearing dilution of the gospel and erosion of our values. The human bomb shelter experience tells me that our *culture of origin* (COO for short) already grips our lives in ways so subtle that Christians may actually embrace them as part of the gospel itself. However, attempting to exorcise the influence of our COO means either trying to live as something we are not (I *am* a suburban, Anglo male, and always will be) or using the look of another culture as the wardrobe for the same heart. This kind of superficial rebadging shows up at every conference I attend in the form of older leaders in buzz cuts and tattoos. Whenever you catch yourself wincing, you're probably looking at one of them. By contrast, missional leaders understand that their COO is only one way of being among many others, with both positive and negative elements; they know that our real "citizenship is in heaven."[3]

The pain of realization shows me the shortcomings and sins of my culture, revealing it as constructed on earth and not received from heaven. This truth allows me to love culture without being owned by it, to say with Paul that "the world has been crucified to me, and I to the world."[4] A missional life, then, means living as an inside-outsider, "not of the world any more than He [Jesus] is of the world."[5] Although the traumas that challenge my cultural paradigms vary greatly, each one affords an opportunity to bring my COO to the cross, revealing its true nature and creating the opportunity for God to renew me by making it more difficult to confuse my culture with His mission.

Fools and Dead Smelt: The Leadership Paradigm

The world we knew in sixth grade did end, but not as a result of a Cold War first strike. A new world gradually replaced it, and the symptoms appeared everywhere. In a recent comparison of traditional technologies with emerging peer-to-peer communication, *Fast Company* contributing editor John Ellis writes, "That idea— that the great all-knowing center broadcasts out to a sea of fools to shape their thoughts and opinions—is as dead as smelt."[6]

Unfortunately, no one bothered to tell me about this. All of my academic and ministerial training prepared me to assume the role of "all-knowing center." I never thought of those I led as a "sea of fools," but I definitely used some synonyms. Completing a Ph.D. in communication studies at Northwestern taught me to think of them as "audiences." Later, in the professional ministry, words such as "members," "volunteers," and "followers" seemed more appropriate somehow. No matter what I called them, my job as the leader was to occupy the center.

My pastoral training included three elements commonly found in my denomination: (1) the experience of growing up in a parsonage, (2) the mentoring influence of an older pastor, and (3) correspondence school studies focusing on the content of the Bible. Entering the ministry in my late twenties, I found this combination served me well, especially in the form of a senior pastor who was willing to take a chance on younger leaders. Under his leadership, our church experienced an exceptional season of growth for which our staff felt largely responsible. After all, we were the center.

In this quite successful situation, my training and experience began converting me into a new sort of insider. This time the influence came not from Cold War suburbia but from the Church that rose up to serve it. I purchased the wire-rimmed glasses, a reddish Bible with twin ribbon markers, and a suit-and-tie combination that resembled those of my favorite television preachers. When I look at photographs of myself from that era, I wonder who I was then, dressed like one of the politicians who give speeches to no one on C-SPAN, dressed in Saul's armor.

My graduate student's jeans and long hair left behind, I conformed to the mainstream of my organization, which viewed such tokens with anxiety and suspicion in those days. (After all, leaders at the center dress as befitting their role.) By way of example, peer pressure, and positive reinforcement, I felt myself melted down and poured into a mold that someone thought represented the ideal pastor, at least in the look-and-feel dimensions. The depression I experienced during this time warned of danger, but I lacked the readiness to listen—yet. In fact, church culture never had a more enthusiastic hostage, the main reason being practical: my training claimed to provide a permanent stockpile of wisdom from which to draw for the rest of my career, guaranteeing a place at the center from which to serve the masses not privy to these divine resources.

Then the real world happened. My wife, Janet, and I assumed our first senior pastorate in a small church, populated largely by baby boomers, in coastal Maine. We experienced the usual trauma that accompanies leaving a somewhat sheltered staff position in a larger congregation for the lead role in a much smaller place. It hurt. But our training equipped us with the strategy that was supposed to produce results. We assumed that this ministry paradigm (three weekly services, fast songs before slow songs, altar calls, holiday musicals) must have God's favor because virtually everyone used it. We arrived in the full expectation that, if we implemented the official tactics, the official results would materialize automatically. We liked the center, because it featured these tidy principles of cause-and-effect.

But our Mainers seemed to have missed a meeting somewhere. An influx of ready-made church members arriving to work at the local shipyard produced growth, but even this ended in a devastating internal conflict that reversed our upward trend. After preaching and praying to almost empty seats during evening services, I finally started to get the message: the ministry formula we were using, the one that kept us at the center, simply failed to function as advertised in this place and time. People of good faith who understood their times developed it, but none of them served here. Until half-way through our tenure, I despaired many days over my congregation's failure to get it; now I understand them as very gracious, giving *me* the time to get it.

Crucified Leadership

The sure and certain knowledge of exactly what to do with a congregation was the most rewarding part of leading from the center. The paradigm involved time-tested principles, with high-profile churches actually offering conferences on how to use them. The thousands of other congregations that struggled while using the same formula got a hearing only as examples of poor execution or weakness in leadership. That worked for me until I became the pastor of one of those congregations and experienced the self-esteem cave-in that accompanies this kind of paradigm crash.

The pain of failure, experienced when I turned off the lights in the empty sanctuary because no one showed up, became another gift. Though my own personal insecurities and limitations were certainly sufficient to avoid success, in the end the grip of the one-size-fits-all paradigm had to be broken by the crisis of declining numbers and church conflict. One afternoon, I sat at my too-big pastor's desk on the second floor of our church building, staring at a pile of brass keys. The keys had two things in common: all of them fit the front door of our church building, and the people who were leaving the congregation during our crisis season placed them all in my hand. I scraped the keys off my desktop into a drawer and closed it.

Burying the church keys in their plywood tomb formed the darkest moment of our first pastoral experience. All of our dreams lay dead, and all our tears and prayers failed to resuscitate them.

The pain masked the fact that failure served me well by crucifying the conceit that I had the ministry figured out and that I was able to administer this model simply by virtue of my office as the source of all wisdom. Jesus did not construct an auditorium and demand that people come to Him. He went to them. Failure challenges the survival of ministry templates that ask culture to meet us on *our* terms. Rather than drawing people to the center, a missional life means Jesus sending us outward, as the Father sent Him.[7]

Eventually, I listened to our congregation enough to understand that they actually needed an informal church, with a light schedule focused on home group activities rather than my sermons. This idea felt almost like heresy, but we did it, and the health of the congregation improved dramatically. I got to know the congregation all over again, my pastoral counseling dropped to almost nothing (it turned out they just needed friends, not me!), and I experienced the joy of having time to pray and study. We experienced more ministry by doing *less*. In fact, the further I moved from the hub, the healthier things seemed to get.

A missional life, then, experiences the centrality of Christ as our failures expose the illusion that we merit the center position. Failure, among other forces, reveals this illusion for what it is, crucifying it and giving us the chance to invite Christ to assume the central role in practice, instead of just in doctrine.

Third Way: The Spirituality Paradigm

If only the lesson had proven enduring. Janet and I moved to coastal Florida, and in our second congregation we served builder generation retirees, immigrants from churches "up North." Having grown up outside their generation and denomination, I struggled to empathize with their nostalgic preference to emulate the Pentecostal worship experiences of the 1960s and 1970s.

After two years of executing the suit-and-tie, three-weekly-services template, I found myself one morning sitting in a pancake eatery in northern Florida, telling Janet that the thought of enduring years of a station-keeping ministry broke my heart. Very few people came to faith, larger churches full of young people outcompeted us for talented members, and stability always trumped my other priorities. What had I become? The reckless Jesus freak of my twenties now looked like a shrink-wrapped, right-from-the-factory, 1980s preacher.

After we finished our pancakes, I yielded to her request that we drive past a church in Pensacola to perform a brief reconnaissance of a congregation experiencing what would come to be called the Brownsville Revival.

Despite my mental (and sometimes verbal) reservations, I found myself immersed in the experience again and again, coming to realize that my own initiative occupied the heart of my ministry. My main vocation focused on maintaining the church culture preferred by our members, and occasionally hoping to secure the board's cooperation for some small tweak. The revival began a season of repenting and realigning our priorities around mission. Janet and I knelt together at a pew in Brownsville, telling the Lord we would do "whatever it takes" to be involved in the real thing, regardless of the cost. This new passion and perspective, and the experiences that accompanied it in those days, met with a mixed response from our congregation, but our focus had changed, and going back held no appeal. We were ruined. Once again the world ended, this time in an old school way: by divine intervention.

Then my denomination offered me a position in our headquarters city of Springfield, Missouri. I accepted, but fifteen months later a congregation in the same city, composed largely of young adults, elected me as their senior pastor. Strongly influenced by the Pentecostal renewal movements of the mid-1990s, our very experiential Sunday services incurred the disdain of some of the religious leadership in the community. But the center no longer had my name on it, and formulas lacked the power over us that they once did. We even made some progress on the look and feel dimension, abandoning suits for corporate casual (radical in that context) and putting everything on a first-name basis.

It was supposed to work. Pentecostals believe in religious experience the way electricians believe in electricity: without it, we have no reason to show up for work. The Spirit moves in profound and observable ways, and our heritage teaches that most everything else just takes care of itself. But our congregation's story failed to line up with what our movement's culture taught us to expect. At one public rally, for example, the only "testimony" from two years of renewal came from one person who thought he might have quit smoking. In my mind, although the renewal brought significant fruitfulness in regard to the worship climate, personal spirituality, and missionary focus of the church, we struggled to identify results in terms of people coming to faith, discipleship, and the like. Was this just another formula, another center? Was my role only to maintain the conditions under which renewal could continue, perpetuating a new version of maintenance church? Even for a naturalized Pentecostal like me, this kind of thinking felt almost treasonous.

Crucified Spirituality

Christians often wait years, or even a lifetime, for the onset of a revival, however defined. After putting in our time, I found myself in this environment, facing a packed auditorium rocking with young adults worshipping God. One particularly dramatic morning service adjourned at 4:30 P.M. But at 4:31, we still faced a long agenda of unsolved problems, and the same questions about tangible fruit. Pentecostal culture sometimes does not permit us to say this out loud, for fear of compromising our emphasis on religious experience as transformational. But I knew the facts of our situation refused to be reduced to experience alone. My naïve faith in unassisted spiritual encounters turned into a search for answers.

The pain of complexity exposes my incomplete understanding of God's ways—the very paradigm most associated with ministers!

Acts 19, for example, tells of Paul meeting disciples at Ephesus who knew only the teachings of John the Baptist and professed total ignorance about the Holy Spirit.[8] Rejecting Paul's teaching and clinging to the repentance-based message of John offered an easy way out. Instead, they opened themselves to a more complex reality and were filled with God's power.

Our congregational culture's tendency to feature experiences disproportionate to results sent me looking for something more. Ironically, Christians assume "more" happens as an inevitable consequence of revival. Soon I heard voices advising even greater experience as the remedy for my problem. But others saw experience as the problem and counseled a healthy dose of pragmatism clothed in suburban respectability. In other words, the conventional wisdom forced me to choose between being a hyper-Pentecostal and an ex-Pentecostal. Both options sounded like substituting a new formula for old.

Living a missional life often means finding a third way, the one outside the boundaries of a facile either-or choice. The hunger for this kind of path brought me into doctoral studies in leadership, which produced a structural overhaul of our church, somehow blending organizational theory with old school intercession. I realized in the process that renewal offers not so much an answer as a question: Why have we been awakened, and what are we prepared to do about that? A third-option church became our answer, one that included a funky, mismatched set of traits reflecting our funky, mismatched collection of gen Xers and senior citizens and the surrounding neighborhood.

We learned the necessity but insufficiency of experience. Few came to faith in our ministry, not because of extremes in our spirituality but because those people seldom attended our services, classes, or anything else. Spiritual seekers in our community simply did not share our assumption that, if a revival broke out at a local church, everyone in town attended. As a result, our spiritual renewal burned brightly in services that only church folks attended and only insiders understood. So with all the best intentions, we succeeded in hosting a more enthusiastic rendition of the center.

It took all of two years to see things begin to change, as we learned how to integrate ministry processes into our understanding of God's power. The exact nature of our revised church is less important than the fact that we embraced a more complex reality in which the ministry moved away from a maintenance mode to a missionary understanding of our role in the city. This transition of perspective drove the changes in the church's structure and ministry. The church started a journey of transformation, in part, because I started the same journey. One Sunday morning, I watched from the pulpit as the first two people indicated their openness to a new faith. With almost no exceptions, I witnessed the same thing every Sunday afterward.

My Best Practice Is Me

In the transition to the missional life through off-road disciplines, my best practice must be *me*. My generation (boomers) tends to look for a better tool, a better model, a better technology, and we have brought this preference into the Church. We like to transform things technologically, thinking of ministry as an instrumentality, ourselves as CEO, the Holy Spirit as a sort of power cell, and the church as an object we modify. In so doing, we risk creating not much more than a hipper version of irrelevance. A missional perspective springs from a transformed interior life that gives us moral authority to lead God's people, "not lording it over those entrusted to you, but being examples to the flock."[9]

It hurts. Realization, failure, and complexity are only examples of the kind of pain signifying that something within me needs to die, that one of my cherished paradigms teeters on the edge of an off-road crash. My culture is unmasked. My methods are neutralized. My assumptions are shattered. In it all, God calls me out of the center that He alone rightfully occupies, to let go of things I treasure, to meet Him among the marginalized where He is always most at work. I will meet Him there most profoundly if the transformation of my inner life is at stake.

Chapter Two

Truth

The Discipline of Sacred Realism

"There aren't any postmodern people in my church!"

An agitated pastor blurted these words at me in a corridor out-side a seminary classroom. Disturbed by course readings on the shifts taking place in our culture, he stalked me and moved in for the kill. I let him ventilate until he started to feel better; then I excused myself from our makeshift therapy session certain of one thing: there *were* no postmoderns in his church.

I encounter the attitude of this pastor, and the condition of his church, regularly. The social mix in which the Church operates bears less resemblance by the day to the setting assumed in our training. Hitting this bump is a sure sign that I am headed off road to face one of the hardest parts of the missional transition.

When I discuss this conclusion with groups of ministers, I get a variety of reactions. Some dismiss me as a diversion from their more practical concerns. Others appear depressed, as if hearing news of the end of the world. An angry minority debate the statistics or, like my stalker, deny the whole scenario. Most of one group just walked out.

Half a decade of field research on the Church in the United States leaves me with the disturbing impression of plateau and decline. This view also represents the consensus of available research and the opinion of the numerous scholars I have consulted in person. For example:

- Telephone surveying finds the number of adults reporting they do not attend church almost doubling since 1991.[1]

- Studies of actual church attendance statistics estimate that only around 17 percent of Americans attend services regularly, far below the rates reported in telephone surveys.[2]

I am aware of the exceptions, the methodological limitations, and the critics of such conclusions. Nonetheless, speaking in broad terms, they represent a truth we cannot ignore. And that's the problem.

The issue becomes what to do with it. Despair and evasion do not seem consistent with Jesus' intention to build His Church.[3] In this chapter, I make the case for another path, the off-road discipline of *sacred realism*. Addressing postmodernism, Christian philosophers often contend for *critical realism*, the notion that absolute truth exists but that our means of knowing suffer from too-human limitations ("Now we see but a poor reflection as in a mirror; then we shall see face to face"[4]).

Sacred realism fearlessly embraces the truth about the Church, and about our lives, because of confidence in a God bigger than those facts. No form of bad news breaks God's grip on our lives or dilutes His love with neutrality. Sacred realism answers the question, "Who shall separate us from the love of Christ?"[5] As we walk in this kind of faith, the truth becomes our friend and never our enemy—although it can feel like the enemy at first.

(412) 731-4063

My father's thriving church served a Pittsburgh suburb that drew its stable, prosperous life from the steel industry in the 1960s. Our city and its culture seemed as permanent as steel, as if upheld by an unspoken social contract between the citizens, the unions, and the mills. Middle- and upper-middle class members living in the neighborhoods around our church, or commuting from first-ring suburbs, filled our sanctuary. Every Sunday, they left their smallish brick houses, down-shifted over the hilly streets, and came to our organ-and-choir services by the hundreds, repeating the cycle the next week. This arrangement was so successful that Calvary Lutheran held double Sunday morning services years before this format gained national popularity.

It was all supposed to endure forever. We were German Lutherans, and this was Pittsburgh. So we demolished a piece of the neighborhood and replaced it with a three-level education complex that housed things like Sunday school classes, basketball games, and square dancing. We served dinners on long folding tables, organized basketball leagues, and performed our version of Broadway musicals. Dedication Sunday for the new facility, with its hardwood gym floor and stainless steel kitchen machinery, was the high-water mark of the church's ministry in the city. Hadrian had his wall; we had our new sandstone brick building.

However, we failed to look out the windows at the surrounding community. On the macro scale, changes in the global economy subverted the reign of Big Steel. Locally, a shifting demographic changed our part of Pittsburgh. The middle class, both black and white, fled the area, exporting prosperous members to second-ring suburbs, too far away for a Sunday morning commute to our city church. Gangs that we thought of as confined to cities such as Los Angeles eventually capitalized on our decline by creating Pittsburgh "franchises." Thirty years after Dedication Sunday, the intersection outside our facility ranked as the number one carjacking location in the city.

Facing the choice of relocating to the suburbs or staying in place, the congregation chose to play defense, the strategy implied by our social contract: we provide the facility and the worship services, and the community supplies the people to fill both. Carefully locked down, the new building evolved into a fortress for our last stand, a Lutheran Alamo. The congregation's unspoken strategy assumed that we could stay in place until our sheer presence wore down both the global economy and local sociology by attrition, bringing a glorious return to the late sixties.

It never happened. Attendance declined throughout the eighties and nineties, and those who remained aged out. The vibrant group of young couples populating the congregation in my boyhood morphed into a staid cohort of senior citizens. The Charismatic Renewal that enlivened the church in the 1970s existed only in memory. In the 1990s, I preached at my father's retirement service with a small, white-haired remnant scattered among the many dozens of dark wood pews. His successors had no better luck.

The denominational authorities attempted to keep this vestige alive in a service held in the church's wedding chapel, while planting a nontraditional congregation in the main sanctuary. Both failed. The funeral for the remnant took the form of an Easter Sunday decommissioning service; the latter met its end less ceremoniously when the church office telephone number was turned off; (412) 731-4063 went silent forever.

I tell the story of Calvary Lutheran not because it is exceptional but because it is not. How have our best efforts come to mean so little to so many?

Wanda and the First Church of Atlantis

Seth invited me to join him for dinner at a Japanese restaurant that served raw food, inviting us to cook our own in wok-like bowls filled with boiling water. We sat on low, swiveling stools at what in another time would have been called a lunch counter, netting boiled pieces of meat and vegetables and then reimmersing them in sauces to supply flavor. Seth recalled that the Japanese military developed this method at some point as a way of keeping troops fed in the field. Somehow it had made its way to Pasadena.

After dinner, we stopped to pay the bill and met Seth's friend, Wanda, the owner of the restaurant. Entirely comfortable in spiritual conversation, he had been building a friendship with her during his stint in the city as a student and businessperson. Seth introduced me immediately: "Wanda, this is Earl. He's a professor of theology, a person who studies about God." She seemed delighted to meet what she called "a God person." Seated behind a small counter, she soon told us about the extremely long hours in the restaurant business and the toll it took on her family, sharing her regrets without hesitation.

We asked Wanda what she thought about God. Her reply was negative. She didn't believe there was a God. So Seth inquired, "Do you pray?" She did, but only when her family was in a crisis. Even then, she said with a laugh, once the emergency abated "We just think it was good luck!" Wanda compared praying to a visit to a family grave: you talk to the tombstone but don't really expect anyone to answer. She went on to voice her preference for the Buddhist approach to prayer, which focuses on peace of mind. By comparison, "Christians just want things." Seth decided to press the issue: "Wanda, what do you think of Christians?" "They vote for Bush," she answered quickly. We thanked her for the good food, paid the check, and, fortified like ancient Japanese soldiers, walked out into the evening in search of the nearest coffee house.

On the sidewalk, I realized that my ministry training and early experiences simply never anticipated a person such as Wanda. She was remarkably open about spiritual things, engaging us in dialogue about God without a hint of discomfort. The stresses and strains of her life opened to our inspection almost immediately. Yet, though Wanda was *spiritually transparent* she was *religiously opaque*. Her compound spirituality took the form

Buddhism + capitalism + emergency prayers + self-reliance
   + pluralism

Compared to Wanda's customized, consumer-friendly package of spiritualities, Christianity appeared unattractive, a religion serving only lazy and self-absorbed Republicans. I concluded that she would be as lost in a conventional church environment as the average conservative evangelical would be in her culture, without an indigenous guide such as Seth. Facing up to Wanda requires courage after investing a lifetime in ministry that assumes a church-friendly audience. She is here, and nothing is going to turn her into the person I was trained to reach.

A Post-Christian Generation

Chip Heath, a professor at the Stanford Business School, writes: "Individuals don't ever go looking for bad news, and we don't like telling it to others. So bad news is unlikely to get to the people who can actually do something about it."[6] The arrival of Wanda was part of the bad news that never reached me during my ministry training. I presumed that those entering my church chose it because they resembled me in important ways. Since I was the center (and all others were to be measured in relation to me), it was only natural to expect to share a similar culture with those I wanted to reach, an article of faith in the Church Growth Movement of the late twentieth century. Then people like Wanda started showing up.

Pastor Daniel Hill defines one source of my presumption by distinguishing between pre-Christians and post-Christians.[7] In general, the pre-Christians tend to be baby boomers with residual memories of church and a neutral-to-mildly-positive nostalgia toward those experiences. The legendary Saddleback Sam, for example, stands as an icon of pre-Christianity. This generation returned to worship in the 1980s and 1990s, bringing their children in tow for Sunday school in the so-called baby boomerang. Pre-Christians helped build the megachurches to which my generation of ministry leaders often looks for inspiration.

Post-Christians tend to be the generation younger than the boomers, packing neutral-to-negative attitudes about organized Christianity that are based on their upbringing outside the church, and their revulsion at its perceived hypocrisy and conservative politics. In fact, the younger the generation, the less likely its members are to be attending.[8] However, post-Christianity defies a simple, generational definition. This group's diversity expresses itself most visibly in an appetite for spirituality in virtually any form.

The Wandas of the world mix Buddhism, capitalism, and just about anything else to form a personal faith, a religion of one. Sarah Michelle Geller (aka Buffy the Vampire Slayer) explains her method: "I consider myself a spiritual person. . . . I believe in an idea of God, although it's my own personal ideal. I find most religions interesting, and I've been to every kind of denomination: Catholic, Christian, Jewish, Buddhist. I've taken bits from everything and customized it."⁹ No wonder we lack icons with names like "Post-Christian Paul," or "Postmodern Paula." By definition, they elude definition.

So, why isn't Wanda coming to church? The History Channel recently offered me part of the answer in a documentary about the researchers who devote their lives to discovering Atlantis. These passionate and sincere people consider themselves consummate professionals in their field. They employ expensive, high-tech equipment and sacrifice the respect of mainstream science to live on the perpetual verge of one of the greatest discoveries of all time. Spurred on by an ancient text (Plato, in this case), they spend years surveying vast stretches of ocean in a quest to assemble clues to cataclysmic events in the distant past. The disdain of their scientific peers only increases their fervor by making these faithful into professional martyrs. Sometime before the last commercial on the TV program, I grasped the parallel to the post-Christian experience of the Church: ancient texts, outrageous theories, huge expense, persecution complex, and a passionate devotion to things that matter only to insiders.

The "First Church of Atlantis" is of declining interest to pre-Christians, and of even less interest to post-Christians. *If we build it, they may not come*. Just saying that out loud feels uncomfortable, perhaps revealing how many of our assumptions appear to resemble the stridency of the Atlantis explorers (or flat-earth proponents) in the eyes of people such as Wanda. Failure to adjust to this cultural gap contributes to the aging out of so many ministries before our eyes. The sense that Atlantis is sinking again definitely worries some of its citizens.

Culture Shock

Missionaries use the phrase *culture shock* to describe the collision of the familiar with the unfamiliar. This expression usually depicts a reaction to some foreign context in which our skills do not function and our social rules no longer apply. I discovered a domestic application of culture shock during a breakfast with Del Tarr, a long-term missionary to West Africa and former seminary president. "What's the difference between truly great missionaries and those who are only average?" I asked. To my surprise, Del began talking about culture shock, about the strain of living and serving outside one's homeland for the first time.

Since the morning of that conversation, I have found myself reminded of Del's account by the Christian leaders I meet at conferences. Missionaries leave their country to face the challenge of adapting to an unfamiliar culture, whereas these men and women stay right here but experience some of the same kind of dislocation. The phases of their culture shock occur in combinations over time, but meeting hundreds of them persuades me that the shock stages generally look something like this:[10]

- *Denial.* The inability to look truth in the eye usually takes two forms. The *logical* type argues with the evidence, claiming that announcing the advent of post-Christianity in this century sounds about like the Y2K predictions of the last. The subtler *cultural* version insinuates that young post-Christians will grow out of it in time, adopting the more conservative attitudes preferred by the center. Even the disciples tried to prevent children from reaching Jesus (perhaps, they thought, when they grow up the little ones will merit some attention, but surely not now).[11] The official prayer of a person in denial might sound something like this: "Lord, stop the mouths of those who are disquieting your people, and restore order to the church so we can return to business as usual, or at least business as I understand it."

- *Anger.* The frustration of our goals, the resentment of being marginalized, or the realization that our assumptions have let us down all contribute to anger. This reaction also appears in two basic forms. The *inward* variety blames the messenger for upsetting the tranquility of the church with paranoid claims. I have become quite familiar with being on the receiving end of this confrontation. The *outward* form of anger drives some Christian leaders to rush to the battlements to defend us from the barbarians at the gates. In presentations, I frequently project the pierced and tattooed face of a young person onto a large screen, usually invoking an audible gasp from the crowd. They recoil instinctively when looking "the enemy" in the eye. (I suppose they think things like this: "How would someone like that look in the choir? What will the board say? What if the youth group all want tattoos?") Their reaction changes when I point out, "If I told you this face came from a developing nation desperately in need of the gospel, you would write me checks to fund missionary work." This new enemy, then, may look odd, hold strangely amorphous beliefs, view a smaller number of truths as absolute, and to some evangelicals seem intent on doing to Christianity what the Visigoths did to Rome.

Almost everyone working through a missional transition spends some time off road in the angry phase. Even the disciples wanted to call down fire on the Samaritan villages that refused to receive their message.[12] So, the person working out her or his anger might pray something like this: "Lord, strike down the enemies of your people, both inside and outside our faith community! Remove the traitors from our midst, and keep the barbarians outside the gates where they belong, so that we are not corrupted by contact with them. Amen."

• *Depression.* Many pastors work hard, doing what they were trained to do, but feel disappointed with the results. For me, among the contributing factors ranks the feeling that my training prepared me for an *endangered context*, leaving me uncertain about my ability to cope. Many older leaders confess to me in private a sense of futility and fear of obsolescence, as if lost on some strange continent. They also tell me of frustration over the lack of outlets for sharing their experience with younger leaders, most of whom they see as rejecting them for displaying a lack of cool. So the prayer of the depressed leader might be: "Lord, I've tried for so long and worked so hard, how could it all have come to this? I went into ministry to save others, and now I need you to save me *from* the ministry. Amen."

- *Bargaining.* I get phone calls and e-mails from pastors who want advice about creating a "gen X service" or "young adult ministry" in their church. The typical caller asks predictable how-to questions but virtually never relates a story of divine guidance into this young-adult initiative. A lot of consulting on these issues, then, leads me to believe that some of what I'm seeing is a form of bargaining. The bargainer's prayer might sound like this: "God, if you'll grow our church as-is, I promise to start a service that appeals to young adults, and to do it at a time and place that won't get me into trouble with the board. Amen." On one level, this plea concerns the need to correct a grave shortage of ministry to young adults. But a new program promoting "relevance" may also function as a preventive to change on a larger scale. In fact, my most disquieting experiences in ministry now spring from events which use me not as a change catalyst but as a change substitute. A friend sensitized me to this paradox when he described organizations that "roll you out to be relevant" and then "put you back on the shelf." For me, that's culture shock.

- *Acceptance.* Living in shock takes too much energy for it to serve as a perpetual state, making acceptance a real possibility in a couple of ways. *Negative acceptance* involves facing the fact that something we are doing needs to be stopped. A large southern church I visited, for example, started a successful young adult ministry that packed a facility across town with twentysomethings soaking up the rock-and-roll worship style. Then the staff decided to evaluate the results of the venture and discovered that Christians made up virtually the whole audience. The senior pastor courageously put the ministry to death on the grounds that the congregation's mission did not include reallocating young Christians in the community. *Positive acceptance*, by contrast, refers to the uncomfortable process of letting the truth spark new strategies that may look nothing like the past. This same church created another young adult ministry with a new leader and a new format that expanded much more slowly but with greater missionary force, attracting a significant number of spiritual seekers. Skipping the negative phase of acceptance could have preempted the positive side from ever materializing. Paul's rejection by the synagogue in Corinth, for example, launched the outreach to the Gentiles that would ultimately bring him to the heart of the Roman Empire.[13]

If the person in acceptance discussed the condition with God, the prayer might be: "Lord, I surrender my place at the center so you can occupy it. Thank you for changing me so that my leadership in mission is worth following. Amen." Both the positive and negative valences of this prayer come from the off-road experience of grasping the reality of our situation while holding on to God, from sacred realism.

Sacred Realism

During our breakfast, Del made the relationship between culture shock and missional effectiveness clear for me. In his experience, there are two ways missionaries respond to the trauma. One reaction blunts the shock with personal toughness and self-reliance. An alternative response resembles a collapse, sometimes plunging the missionary into a season of near-despair compounded by the practical challenges of the first stint overseas. This breaking of the will is a unique opportunity to relinquish control and turn to God as sustainer, creating sensitivity to His voice and empathy for others. The process begins with a question: "Who is equal to this task?"[14] "Not me," replies the missionary. The phases of culture shock transform this simple fact into a lived reality, into a sacred realism grasping insufficiency and God's utter competence simultaneously.

On a congregational level, the good people of Calvary Lutheran grew up in a world in which 75 percent of us Americans attended worship and more than 80 percent of us practiced the religion of our parents. The fault lines that were fracturing this world were so outside our experience that culture shock drove the congregation deeper into itself. The search for Atlantis continued, while the Wandas of their community largely missed the opportunity to consider what George Hunter calls "the Christian possibilities" for their lives. The same response to culture shock is neutralizing too many ministries today.

Post-Christianity is waiting for missionaries who practice sacred realism: the discipline of holding the truth in one hand and faith in the other. Neither fatalism nor mindless optimism amounts to an acceptable alternative. The courage to face uncomfortable realities about myself and my setting comes from the recognition that God's hand manifests itself in every reality. Most of us think about how we can change culture. Sacred realism gives culture a chance to change us.

Chapter Three

Perspective

The Discipline of POV

The maroon Honda Accord stood out among the other used cars on the corner lot in Chicago. As a Japanese import, just catching on in the late 1970s, the vehicle packed a hidden irony. Its previous owner was the Ford Motor Company. What motivated the Ford people to buy a Honda? Almost certainly, they wanted to find out what made Hondas work and why so many Americans liked to buy them. In this pursuit, the Ford engineers probably raced the thing around a track for days, took it apart, scrutinized it, blueprinted it, put it back together, and then resold it—to me.

This process of reverse engineering aims to back a design out of something that already exists (say, a Honda), rather than using what I call "blueprint" engineering, in which design principles are used to diagram a new product in hopes that a functioning proto-type (like a Ford) actually works. In the science fiction film *Paycheck*, for example, a reverse engineer played by Ben Affleck seeks to learn the inner workings of new technologies so secret that he agrees, for a huge fee, to have his memory erased at the end of every job. Whether an industrial spy or a conventional product designer, all reverse engineering seeks to learn so much from things as they *are* that things as they *can be* have a chance to emerge. Perhaps the Fords of the late seventies improved marginally because of the autopsy performed on my Honda.

Christian mission tends to prefer a blueprint point of view (POV) that insists on replicating designs developed in a relative vacuum, or cloning methods used somewhere else. An almost end-less series of conferences and catalogues offer leaders the resources that claim to do this. For years, the bottom shelf of my study book-case was home to a four-inch thick, three-ring binder that held an acquaintance's master plan for revolutionizing any church, complete with three-dimensional diagrams and fill-in-the-blank forms (just like those used by Paul and Peter). A reverse engineering POV applied to Christian mission starts with the off-road discipline of interpreting culture (the equivalent of disassembling the Honda) and arrives at a strategy for mission as its deliverable. The reverse engineering POV recognizes that a teenage devotee of Manga comics hears the gospel differently from a thirtysomething advertising executive, or a middle-aged English literature professor. This chapter argues that, in part, postmoderns have it right: POV is everything, and one of the most useful ways to develop a missional POV is to back it out of culture.

Postmodernism may pose one of the trickiest reverse engineering challenges of our era. How do you disassemble a worldview about which one observer quipped, "The word has no meaning. Use it as often as you can."[1] In addition to definition, postmodernism also seems to lack synonyms. This challenge motivates a small army of writers, among them evangelicals, who build careers defining, analyzing, lauding, and decrying the "postmodern turn."

Debate even rages over the nature and the scale of this shift. Theologian Paul Elbert complains about "the unsubstantiated assumption that the world in which we evangelize is somehow delineated by 'postmodernism' ";[2] missiologist Craig Van Gelder blithely refers to it as "the cultural air we breathe."[3] Almost everyone agrees, however, that something new is happening around and among us. I know of few ideas that elicit such a range of interpretation, producing a virtual cottage industry. Several reverse engineering models mark the phases of my own attempt to understand the implications of postmodernism for Christian mission. Each takes the form of a question asked by my professional peers at stages of my travels, as they tried to sort out what exactly it is that I do. Driving to O'Hare Airport one day, with Len Sweet crammed into the back seat of my red Mazda, I described this identity confusion and received some good advice: "Don't give it a name; if you name it, you'll try to control it." So I am left with the questions.

Aren't You the Postmodernism Guy?

Many academic disciplines devote attention to the postmodern, often depicting it as a popular rejection of modern, technological rationalism. Postmoderns turn away, the argument goes, from what they perceive as modernity's optimistic brand of malevolence, a culturally vapid force at best (shopping at The Gap), and a globally destructive impulse at worst (children in sweatshops making jeans for The Gap). Since postmodernism refers to many things, it seems to enjoy a Teflon coating, with all attempts at ultimate categorization simply slipping off, leaving the definition in the eye of the beholder.

My initial foray into these issues focused on this conundrum of defining the philosophy—or was it a worldview, or an era, or just a mood? Part of my motivation developed out of advice received from a trusted friend while considering my job change into academic administration. He counseled me that my denomination lacked a "postmodernism guy," and that assuming this role almost guaranteed an identity, a personal brand. He was right. So, working in the world of ideas, I assumed that conferring a concrete meaning on the word (the sort that makes good lecture material) might also concretize some missional options.

Several years of research brought me to a reverse engineering solution in the form of a metaphor: the black hole. These gravity wells in deep space pull in everything under their influence, including light itself, forming a point of infinite density at their heart. For postmodern philosophy, the question of whether anything can be known throbs at the center of this epistemological black hole. The closer to the center of the black hole, the more definitive the answer: "No!" The farther from the depths of the well, the more equivocal the answer, yet the gravitational pull of no never completely disappears, influencing everything within its grasp.

At its heart, postmodernism is a philosophy of no. Nothing can be known because everything we think of as reality depends on our interpretation and expression of it. Truth, then, is a hostage of our point of view and the arbitrariness of the sounds we organize into language. The singularity created by these forces leads to total rejection of all certainty at its core, a selective suspicion in what I call the "midrange," and a superficial effect on look-and-feel issues at the outer rim. The university English major, for example, who has been persuaded that all communication is merely "text" and has come to doubt the reality of everything but interpretation lives near the point of infinite density. Meanwhile, a student in the same classroom may embrace a certain cynicism about powerful institutions but reject as absurd and impractical the notion that nothing can be known. (The existence of a midterm exam offers all the reality the second student needs.) A third student seated nearby may care little for either philosophy or power analysis but greatly admire the affectations (fashion, media) of postmodernism as a culture. All three students are in the grip of the gravity of no, with varying degrees of intensity and awareness. So the philosophy affects those under its influence according to their closeness to the ultimate no.

Proximity to this core produces assumptions like "incredulity toward metanarrative"[4] (no one story explains all our individual stories), the arbitrariness of both language and truth, and the use of communication by the powerful as an instrument—a weapon—of oppression. Disclosing these strategies of deceit and giving voice to those at the margins through deconstruction (a favorite activity of postmoderns) is one of the primary benefits (and major gravitational attractions) of postmodern theory. Abuse of power and use of media for deception are common enough in our world to make some forms of deconstruction necessary and popular, even among those who have never heard the word. On a personal level, those influenced strongly by the philosophy's pull tend to resent efforts to label them as a certain kind of person. Near the singularity, the point of infinite uncertainty, even human beings cannot be truly known, and any protestation to the contrary represents just another form of oppression—you defining me. No. No. No.

The scholarly POV offers benefits to a mostly ingrown church that needs to hear voices from communities that do not share its agenda. Academic work in philosophy and literary theory helps us dig beneath superficial and sometimes distracting cultural cues (such as tattooing) to access the assumptions on which millions of people live their lives without ever hearing the P word. As Christian philosophers Jon Hinkson and Greg Ganssle explain, "Few people consciously adopt all the views of either Foucault or Rorty or any other thinker. Most people hold a hybrid view that is picked up from various sources along the way without much critical reflection."[5] The academic POV uniquely interprets the major thinkers of the postmodern turn and in so doing helps us understand which ideas and behaviors are significant for the ministry of the Church.

In a free market of ideas that tests explanations against each other, the Church learns and grows—if we pay attention. However, in a survey of magazine indices I found that the first references to *postmodernism* in Christian periodicals did not appear until four to thirteen years after the first references are indexed in secular journals. With this sort of culture lag in place, the path forward will not be paved with journal articles.

Whenever a conference audience or class asks me to define postmodernism, I often laugh out loud. "If we can only capture this thing in a sentence," they assume, "perhaps accompanied by an example or two, then we'll be ready to do something about it!" Usually, I make reference to a world without a center, a philosophy that has the essential trait of having no essential trait, or the transition from Ozzie and Harriet to Ozzy and Sharon. But none of these remarks constitute, even in combination, a depiction of this philosophical black hole any more than a few images from the Hubble space telescope capture every critical aspect of a gravity well. To do mission, we need more.

Aren't You the Culture Guy?

The early response of scholars to postmodernism pertained largely to the world of ideas, with evangelicals citing Nietzsche as a primary source of a radical nihilism lurking at the heart of the black hole. Realizing the tangible, but limited, benefits of these interpretations, I felt the pull toward a more cultural point of view that seeks to answer a simple question: How is postmodernism influencing the way people actually live? In other words, do postmodern ideas translate at all into postmodern culture? In pursuit of answers, some within our fellowship began to refer to me rightly or wrongly as "the culture guy."

The first cultural theory I encountered announced what I would call a *stock market crash*. Advocates of this position believe that modernism's collapse started sometime in the middle of the twentieth century, losing much of its value in the culture and clearing the way for a hostile takeover by postmodernism. "Modernism is crumbling,"[6] Baptist pastor Robert A. Weathers laments. From his vantage point, postmodernism's victory is near-total and permanent: "It's here. It's reality. It's the future." Refusal to face the harsh reality of the "crash" is analogous to insisting that the earth is the center of the solar system or that the earth is flat.

Crash theorists draw on the distinction between philosophical and cultural postmodernism to failsafe their position. In a 2001 interview, the late theologian Stanley Grenz contended that, even if the more philosophical brand of postmodernism declines, "there is no going back from many of the intellectual sensitivities that characterize the postmodern ethos. These include such hallmarks as the dethroning of reason in favor of a more holistic understanding of the human person, the rejection of radical individualism in favor of a more communitarian understanding of existence, and the rejection of uniformity in favor of the celebration of difference."[7]

A second example of cultural POV is what I call the *rearview mirror* model, which trumps crash theory by agreeing with postmodernism's impact but framing the shift as having a very short shelf life. The argument for a temporary cultural turn finds support in the nature of postmodernism itself. Os Guinness, a primary exponent of this view, states bluntly, "I don't think postmodernism will be around in ten years' time." He contends that an essentially negative philosophy is unsustainable because it offers no resources with which to "build a family, sustain a university, or run a country."[8] An even more impatient variant of this theory argues for post-postmodernism, on the basis of the increasingly positive attitudes and behaviors of the under-thirty generation. Drawing on brightening media images of young adults, writer and worship expert Sally Morgenthaler writes, "Twentysomething rage and cultural dismantling—so hip just an eye-blink ago—now seem as musty as Woodstock on Memorex or Sarah Brighton on PBS."[9] Advocates of the rearview mirror definitely represent the minority report on the subject, but their influence is growing.

Even the rearview mirror interpretation proves too strong for the advocates of what I call the *Y2K model,* which contends that cultural changes do not add up to a postmodern turn; it simply never happened in the United States. Like the end of civilization expected on New Year's Day 2000, or the advent of the metric system, or the announcement of cold fusion, postmodernism generates a lot of paranoia (especially among evangelicals) but just never actually shows up, at least in America. In *Soul Searching,* for example, the largest study of American teen spirituality ever conducted, Christian Smith argues that "our findings suggest to us that religious communities should also stop . . . presuming that U.S. teenagers are actively alienated by religion, are dropping out of their religious congregations in large numbers, cannot relate to adults in their congregations, and so need some radically new 'postmodern' type of program or ministry. None of this seems to us to be particularly true."[10] For Smith, thousands of surveys and hundreds of interviews disclosed a postmodern turn that happened often in the ivory tower but seldom in high school.

Trying to make sense of these competing theories complicates any sort of cultural understanding. For example, I have conducted informal polls among hundreds of secular university undergraduates, asking them how often they hear the word *postmodernism* on campus. With the exception of the English literature majors, they answer, "Just about never." Does this mean the reversal of the postmodern turn, or that it never occurred in the first place? Perhaps. More likely, it means that university culture feels the pull of the philosophy so completely that saying the word is no more necessary than mentioning gravity.

So I decided to form a cultural POV that assumed the validity of all three theories, but not necessarily at the same time or in the same place. This assumption led me to another metaphor: the Torino Scale.[11] Late in the last century, some scientists claimed that our world's orbit around the sun came perilously close to the path of a planet-smashing asteroid. The kind of rock that annihilated the dinosaurs was hurtling on its way to kill all of us too. A buildup in the media ultimately led to the discovery of flawed mathematics in the projections of a near-miss. The earth was saved—but then, it was never really in danger. Disaster of the sort portrayed in the films *Deep Impact* and *Armageddon* just never happened, but the idea of near-earth asteroids got everyone's attention.

Astronomers gauge an asteroid's threat to the earth using the Torino Scale. With eleven levels ranging from "zero or virtually zero chance of impact" to "certain collision causing global climactic catastrophe," the scale portrays the relative likelihood of an apocalyptic collision and its aftermath. Several years of field work in emerging culture persuade me that the arrival of postmodernity resembles a Torino event. Some people and places seem to avoid the impact virtually altogether (for now), while other regions and demographics have experienced a cultural cataclysm.

Touring the streets of Amsterdam or Copenhagen, and walking neighborhoods such as Deep Ellum in Dallas, Uptown in Minneapolis, or Pearl Street in Boulder, I find deep craters, evidence of impact rating a Torino 10. Much of modernity's scientific optimism reached extinction in these areas long ago. Yet both survey data and

The Torino Scale	
0	Zero or virtually zero chance of impact
1	Impact extremely unlikely, merits monitoring
2	Impact very unlikely
3	Close encounter with at least 1% chance of local destruction
4	Close encounter with at least 1% chance of regional destruction
5	Close encounter with significant threat of regional destruction
6	Close encounter with significant threat of global catastrophe
7	Close encounter with extremely significant threat of global catastrophe
8	Certain collision with local destruction
9	Certain collision with regional devastation
10	Certain collision causing global climatic catastrophe

personal experience tell me millions of us refuse to believe that truth is constructed, or that language is pure contrivance, or that values have no source outside the human beings who invent them. (Ironically, this trait unites people of faith with scientific secularists in a common aversion to the postmodern black hole.) Of course, a large middle area between 0 and 10 makes up most of the Torino scale, representing people feeling postmodernism's influence (perhaps in religious pluralism) but simultaneously clinging to a modern perspective to some degree (even the most devout pluralist is optimistic about penicillin).

Taking these dynamics into consideration, applying the Torino Scale to the likelihood of a postmodern impact on the life of one person might look something like this:[12]

0. Zero or virtually zero chance of postmodern influence in our lifetime (example: the Torino family are Christian fundamentalists living in a "red" state, speaking in terms of U.S. politics)

1. Impact extremely unlikely, but merits monitoring (Nick Torino is a home-schooled child)

2. Impact very unlikely (Andy Torino is a public-schooled child)

3. Close encounter with at least 1 percent chance of local influence (Andy leaves home to attend a red-state Bible college after a summer youth camp experience)

4. Close encounter with at least 1 percent chance of regional influence (tired of rules, Andy transfers to a red-state Christian liberal arts university; youth camp was a long time ago)

5. Close encounter with significant threat of regional influence (still tired of rules, and wanting a more prestigious degree, Andy transfers to a blue-state secular university)

6. Close encounter with significant threat of global influence (Andy chooses English major in secular university, over parents' objections)

7. Close encounter with extremely significant threat of global influence (Andy learns deconstruction and "hermeneutic of suspicion" from favorite English professor)

8. Certain impact with overwhelming local influence (Andy moves off campus to nearby artsy neighborhood)

9. Certain impact with overwhelming regional influence (Andy discontinues sporadic church attendance, preferring companionship and acceptance in local coffee houses)

10. Certain impact by postmodernism causing cultural and paradigmatic catastrophe (Andy tells the other Torinos, "I don't know how I could ever have believed all that stuff")

I conclude that the influence of postmodernism is, well, relative; we take the postmodern turn at different speeds. Some of the impact depends on *where* you are (my mother's kitchen or a coffee house in Seattle), some on *who* you are (a middle-class Anglo male versus a female college student), and some on your *culture* of origin (landline telephones and mimeograph machines; blogging and podcasting). As Craig Van Gelder notes, "the hypermodern and the postmodern are now layered within the ongoing reality of modernity."[13] I call this layered world "Postmodernia"—a continent, like the Internet, with a citizenry but not necessarily a geography. The key questions for the church change as soon as we set foot on this new continent. Rather than asking, "Should we play U-2 songs during our worship services?" missional thinkers start asking more disturbing questions: "Which worldview does the church represent? Which reality does the church seek to engage through mission?"[14]

Where Are You a Missionary to?

Definitions are important. If an asteroid is approaching, we do need to know both its size and its course. But neither precise word meanings nor astronomical analogies suffice. Descriptions of postmodernism as an X somehow distinct from modernity (the holy grail of the scholarly POV) and video clips depicting its social symptoms (the most prominent artifact of the cultural POV) both merit our attention. However, translating even the best of these insights into actual mission proves disturbingly difficult. Perhaps the explanation is just as plain as Internet pastor Tim Bednar's blunt statement in a 2005 blog: "The problem is that most postmoderns would rather die than have the church (or God) meet their needs."[15]

Proclaiming the Kingdom of God among the citizens of Postmodernia requires more than just philosophical analysis and cultural sensitivity—both of which are assets a well-educated atheist could supply. An additional POV seems called for. Visiting a church during a missions-emphasis weekend I attended, person after person (who recognized me as a guest with a necktie) asked the same question: "Where are you a missionary to?" Where indeed? The more appropriate question in postmodernity seems to be "*Who* are you a missionary to?" Reducing people to their geography serves the mission (and the people) as badly as reducing them to their worldview or musical preferences. The Father did not send Jesus to redraw maps, or refine worldviews, or redeem music. He came for people, spiritual beings who sin and hurt and die.

A missional POV on the citizens of Postmodernia begins with Jesus' point of view on Himself: "the Son of Man came to seek and to save what was lost."[16] Postmoderns (and premoderns, and moderns!) are not philosophers in need of enlightenment or rock stars seeking a gig; they are human beings searching for the transcendent. Since the postmodern preferences for diversity and tolerance tend to repel dependence on a monolithic religion, the path to the spiritual may involve compound spiritualities, sometimes side by side with formal religion. In this sense, a person high on the Torino scale may express citizenship in Postmodernia not by rejecting all truth but by embracing every spiritual option as equally true—at least for now.

Former missionary and church planting expert Gailyn Van Rheenen relates the experience of Julie, a devotee of compound spirituality:

Linda, a member of the First Christian Church, practices Reiki therapy (the Japanese art of therapeutic touch) in my hometown. I met Linda on the day that she decided to go public concerning her involvement with folk religion. Her speech, given at an occult fair, was entitled "Can You Be a Christian and a Psychic? Yes!" When a prayer partner and I entered the room for the presentation, she turned from those with whom she was conversing and to our surprise said, "I perceive that one of you is a preacher." During her presentation, she led participants through a personality profile to enable them to ascertain whether they had the spiritual propensities to be clairvoyants, clairaudients, intuitives, and prophets. She then equated these psychic abilities to the gifts of the Holy Spirit in

1 Corinthians 12. Later I asked two graduate students to interview Linda. They found that Linda began her training in Reiki by going through an "attunement" in which she was "opened to the flow of Reiki energy." During this attunement experience, Linda received what she called "the gift of vision." Each time she conducts her Reiki therapy with a client she sees images of light. These have vague human form but are not distinct. Lacking a better name, Linda calls these figures her "light workers." While believing in God and salvation in Jesus Christ on a cosmic level, Linda uses therapeutic touch and meditation to heal, relax, and rejuvenate both herself and her patients.[17]

Linda's story is being repeated millions of times over, suggesting that Postmodernians are not so much practicing a philosophy as they are a folk religion, an informal blend of spiritualities and religious options that suit the needs of the moment. These informal spiritualities claim to do things (tranquility, healing, addiction recovery) for their adherents that they doubt more institutional forms of religion are able to do.

Whether dealing with the negative, angst-ridden European version or its more positive, pragmatic American cousin (which I call McPostmodernism), adopting a folk religion POV changes things for missional people. First, this perspective serves as a powerful reminder of what mission to Postmodernia is *not*. Standing outside the gate of the Christiania community in the heart of Copenhagen, Denmark, a local church leader confessed to me his fear of engaging this libertarian enclave in which the sign marking the main thoroughfare says "Pusher Street." Despite the impressive numerical growth of the ministry he represented, his face reflected the anxiety and guilt of other leaders who privately confess to me their hesitation over connecting with Postmodernians. They waver not so much from anger or judgment as from fear. Adding the folk religion POV to the mix encourages leaders to greater dependence on spiritual resources such as prayer, faith, and love to bring down spiritual strongholds, recognizing we wrestle "not against flesh and blood,"[18] even on the Internet. The effectiveness of Christian mission among folk religionists around the world is well established. Why assume we must be less effective among spiritual pluralists in North America?

Tiempos Mixtos

We live in *tiempos mixtos*, mixed times in which modern, premodern, and postmodern expressions swirl together in the same social space. My navigation of this perfect storm began with the goal of defining postmodernism but led to the conclusion that the list of things the word does *not* mean might be shorter. So I moved on to the issue of postmodern culture, hopefully gaining some sensitivity to the nuances lost when only defining a word. But converting that knowledge into the kind of wisdom needed to guide mission proved daunting.

Today, I work at understanding the folk religion POV that frames postmodernism as a spiritual force to be reckoned with in spiritual terms. Hopefully, working out of a spiritual perspective cultivates more radical dependence on God's power as the indispensable ingredient of mission to all people in all places: "For the kingdom of God is not a matter of talk but of power."[19] After all, modernity is not the pivot of history; the cross is.

Moreover, a spiritual framework properly conceived actually invites both the scholarly and the cultural POVs to be part of the mix as servants of God's mission. The American Church relies so much on leadership skills and ministry methodologies that I wonder if dependence on God's power doesn't constitute the last option most of the time, producing an experience so shallow that confidence (or do I need to say *faith?*) in God's abilities never reaches critical mass. A few trips through Postmodernia might be just what we need.

Chapter Four

Learning

The Discipline of Reverse Mentoring

Tom, the celebrity guest speaker, taunted us: "How many people are *you* mentoring right now?" The conference room grew quieter as the ˏ ile on his face broadened. The seventy-five or so people who were gathered to eat croissant sandwiches while learning leadership principles from Tom ran calculations silently in their heads.

"I'm mentoring *seventeen!*" he blurted out after a dramatic pause, clearly relishing the opportunity to make this number a matter of public record. With his credentials established (at least in his own mind), the audience began telegraphing approval to Tom using the quiet murmur of the medium-size group. I suspect the majority's surprisingly favorable reaction stemmed from their resonance with a certain definition of mentoring that Tom represented, as depicted in films such as *The Karate Kid,* in which an older expert (Mr. Miyagi) teaches martial arts to a novice, Daniel.[1] Mr. Miyagi's ability to defeat Daniel almost effortlessly in any form of hand-to-hand combat qualified him as the mentor. In fact, the 1984 film's tagline is, "Only the 'Old One' could teach him the secrets of the masters."

What if this film inspired a remake today in the context not of martial arts but of martial arts video gaming? Facing Daniel on an Xbox, Mr. Miyagi's position as mentor could not survive the first clash. As Garrett, a midtwenties church staffer, told me, "I can beat people just a couple years older than me in video games with no trouble because I started younger. It's like learning a language. It's a lot easier when you're young." Garrett elaborated: "You could play Xbox two hours a day for months, and a nine-year-old could beat you on his first day." Ouch. As far as this language goes, I speak an outmoded dialect, and just about anyone younger knows it.

If, in some ways, the Xbox now represents our culture more accurately than face-to-face combat, mentoring relationships assume a complexity beyond that of Mr. Miyagi and Daniel, or Yoda and Luke Skywalker. The Xbox factor changes everything. As the *Economist.com* points out, "The Internet has triggered the first industrial revolution in history to be led by the young. . . . The old premium on maturity, from the age-based seniority of the office to the uniforms of adulthood, is disappearing."[2] The stress of this transition is portrayed in the movie *In Good Company*, by Dennis Quaid as Dan Foreman, an aging advertising executive demoted and forced to work for Topher Grace (as Carter Duryea), a much younger and hipper boss. Dan believes in long-term relationship building and handshake deals, while Carter preaches the gospel of "synergy." Their tortured, but ultimately fruitful, relationship speaks to both the pain and the potential that Xbox culture presents for older leaders.

Tapping the wisdom of the young requires that missional leaders go off road to develop *reverse mentoring* (R-mentoring) relationships, a very specific form of friendship in which the junior instructs the senior, not as a replacement for other forms of mentoring but as an essential complement to them. This chapter argues the necessity of R-mentoring on the basis of the logic of the Xbox, and on my own experience with dozens of R-mentors, the young leaders who have trained me for the last five years.

Led by such large firms as General Electric and Procter & Gamble, the corporate world uses R-mentoring routinely for two good reasons: it works, and the alternative spells technological obsolescence.[3] Any midlife adult asking a twelve-year-old for help with a computer problem uses exactly the same reasoning as these multinational corporations. In fact, a Carnegie Mellon study of home computer use found the "family tech guru" is now most likely an adolescent—or younger.[4] In the context of the missional life, Timothy still needs Paul, but Paul now needs Timothy.

www.IDontGetIt.com

My mother recently asked a devastating question: "Earl, what *is* the Internet?" I had no words. How do I explain the Internet to a very smart person (a valedictorian) who worked with computers only near the end of her professional career? It's not that she couldn't understand it. My crisis arose from the question's very existence, one that forced me to wonder how *my* queries come across to the young.

For example, when I asked a group of young staff pastors a couple years ago, "Why would anyone want to send a text message, *anyway?*" their blank expressions melted into laughter, telling me that my new Internet address should be something like www .IDontGetIt.com. Even worse, the tone of my inquiries probably sounds to them like a tourist trying to achieve understanding in another country by speaking very loudly and very slowly: "WHERE . . . IS . . . THE . . . BAAATHHHH . . . ROOOOOOM??!!"

Out of kindness, my R-mentors try to conceal their reactions to my clumsiness, but their nonverbal cues seldom lie: I am from the planet 8-Track and they live on a world called iPod.

Ironically, sometimes clumsiness pays off handsomely. I simply stumbled into most of my R-mentoring relationships, having never heard the phrase nor read a word about it. Anyone drawn to the missional life finds that sacred accidents like this happen with encouraging regularity. Perhaps the first of these surprised us while Janet and I were pastoring a mostly young adult church. My wife began to approach the young women in the congregation for fashion advice (which in those days was mainly about wearing black) as a way of building relationships with them. Through Janet's conversations and many of my own with our several hundred twentysomethings, we began to see the error of our assumption that they represented a junior version of us, destined to grow up into baby boomers. Relationship gave us a new picture of young adults as in many ways a different species: *Homo postmodernus*.[5]

We found them fascinating, likeable, and excellent teachers. They took us in and began to give us the guided tour of their lives on the iPod home world. We discovered immediately that our young tutors enjoyed what academics call "tacit knowledge," an enormous stock of data and experience not yet communicated—at least to us.[6] They possessed, for example, an encyclopedic knowledge of good coffee and Indy rock music, and a strong preference for "hanging out" as the basic platform for all ministry. We found them willing to share it with anyone who asked—even old people like us—as long as we listened instead of talked.

Our church began to make sense only as we helped the natives unpack their tacit knowledge in ways that served to guide the ministry. When conventional Sunday school classes proved to be of limited interest, for example, our leadership team heard the twentysomethings (who thought of 9:00 on Sunday morning as the middle of the night) expressing enthusiasm about the possibility of evening home meetings. The first one grew to forty to fifty people (several times larger than the boomer playbook allows) and then spun off other meetings of similar size, growing a larger Sunday school class in the process. They had it right. The playbook had it wrong.

Experiences like these shifted some of our definitions. Previously, I understood my role as knowing important things, and their role as receiving those things from me. Now, I admitted the truth: they knew important things too, and part of my job revolved around grasping those things by way of relentless listening. We arrived at the church to save the natives, but the natives saved us.

The hundreds of younger leaders I meet during travel and field research continue this pattern, with many of them offering me invaluable native wisdom through R-mentoring. They are my instructors. Although I also mentor some of them, turning to those much younger than me affords a kind of training unavailable in any other way. Simply spending time with them helps me understand their customs and their assumptions at a level that formal education could never match.

Here are just a few examples of R-mentors at work in my own life, illustrating some of how they enrich everything I do:

• *Texting.* Justin, Andrea, Dan, Rachel, and Bryan, my friends at the Oaks Fellowship near Dallas, spent considerable time one evening at an IHOP teaching me to send text messages on my cell phone (with its ancient green screen). Texting for the first time was a thrill (I now know how pets feel when they are taught tricks). I forgot how to find the text command on that phone only hours later, but I located it on my next model because I listened to the *logic* (that is, how to use the menus) of texting at the IHOP. The information helped, but their perspective also drew me inside the world of the texter, and her or his view of information as a process rather than just a commodity. As a result, when speaking to millennial audiences, I now request that they text at least one time during my presentation, asking only that the message pertain to our subject in some way. This option defies every particle of my communication training, all of which assumes the 8-track context. On iPod, if they are not texting they are not listening. For them, lateral (P2P—person to person) communication is as natural as vertical (broadcast-style) communication is to me.

• *PowerPoint.* After hearing a talk supported by PowerPoint, Glen (half my age) said politely, "I thought you had a degree in communication." This gift of the truth taught me the difference between effective use of PowerPoint (a technology I had only recently learned to misuse) and the kind of slide shows that get people laughing in the car on the way home. Several years later, a group of Xbox natives revealed an even more profound insight. From their perspective, PowerPoint represents only an old person's futile (and pathetic) attempt to look technologically current. While Glen's comment shocked me out of my "wall 'o text" mind-set, the observations of other young leaders challenged me to reconsider the whole idea of using PowerPoint and to think not so much about creating slides as about creating understanding. My use of PowerPoint today operates under three rules: (1) don't, (2) be minimalist, use my own photography, and (3) use video instead.

These small examples document that knowing the natives trumps just knowing *about* them. Personal relationships access not just their knowledge (how not to develop a PowerPoint presentation) but their point of view (why PowerPoint looks like "cheese" to under-thirties). In combination, these two elements tune us into the most important part of a culture, the unspoken assumptions that natives understand tacitly.

Justin (also half my age), for example, told me about the rules that producer Larry David gave the writers of the *Seinfeld* program: "no hugging, no learning." I immediately Googled the phrase and found confirmation that these two principles guided both the plot and the dialogue of every episode yet were never articulated outright by any of the characters. Similarly, the cultures of which we are all a part are shaped by powerful, but unspoken, assumptions without which they would lose their identity. From the moment of Justin's revelation, I never saw *Seinfeld* in the same way again, since I could not unknow the rules. Each half-hour still made me laugh, but now I knew why. I got it. A *Homo postmodernus* reverse mentor can help me understand the unpublished assumptions of that culture in the same way, offering me access to the rules operating behind the scenes so I have a better opportunity to shape ministry that makes sense to people, much as our oversize home meetings made sense to our young adults. Meeting in homes sent a message about being part of a family that the boomer playbook knew nothing about. Corporations see the value of accessing tacit knowledge and now routinely require their marketing and sales personnel to engage in reverse mentoring sessions with those young enough to intuit the dynamics of emerging markets. What makes us think we can skip this step?

Planned Dis-Obsolescence

Asking someone half your age and of less seniority (and perhaps less reputation and influence) for advice and instruction is profoundly humbling. If there were no other benefits, this sanctifying experience in and of itself recommends R-mentoring. In fact, Wharton School professor Jerry Wind contends that "embarrassment" by the senior member of the relationship often represents the biggest barrier to allowing "upward mentoring" to function effectively.[7] Even if the insights gained prove less-than-useful (always a live option), the act of asking for help always serves us well. Humility is wisdom's constant companion, or, as Alvin Taylor puts it, "In the twenty-first century, an illiterate is not one who cannot read or write, but one who is unwilling to learn, unlearn, and relearn."[8]

So, how does the kind of upward mentoring involved in this off-road discipline take concrete form in the missional life?

Reality

My age and my "get it" quotient (GIQ) are inversely related. The high school student working the counter at McDonald's one fateful Sunday morning offered me (unsolicited) my first senior citizen's discount on a cup of bad coffee. She knew me better than I knew myself, in that my mind still feels nineteen years old and still thinks that I "get it." When I am asked what I read to stay culture-current, I confess that no amount of information adds up to relevance in the way meant by the question. No one has invented the hardware that can make me get it. I am by nature *Homo modernus*, and I will get it less and less as the years pass.

I must confess to bouts of roiling anxiety and defensiveness that come with the sense that my own indigenous modernist culture, or "situational geography,"[9] is receding to the trailing edge. Despite our protestations, *Homo modernus* becomes less and less formative of our culture every day (except as voting members of AARP), replaced by techno-savvy *Homo postmodernus* young people who bring skill sets far beyond just the Xbox. Alan Webber, the cofounder of *Fast Company*, puts it this way: "It's a situation where the 'old fogies' in an organization realize that by the time you're in your forties and fifties, you're not in touch with the future in the same way as the young twenty-somethings. They come with fresh eyes, open minds, and instant links to the technology of our future."[10] Failing to develop learning relationships within this context holds me hostage to my own situational geography and tacit knowledge, both of which started clocking out a long time ago. No one cares today about my working knowledge of the IBM Selectric typewriter, a miracle machine just twenty-five years ago.

The choices become plain: (1) *ignore* Xbox culture and say (as a conference participant recently informed me in a Q&A session), "If we just follow the Holy Spirit, we don't really need to know all of this"; (2) *pretend* to have a high GIQ by assuming the affectations of the young (untucked shirts, hip-hop fashion, or whatever look pleads "I get it!" at the time); or (3) simply *admit* the truth that my GIQ declines by the hour and that I need instruction from younger people.

Spirituality

Reverse mentoring involves a specific form of friendship based on trust. Mentoring comes in many forms (downward, peer-to-peer, upward) and formats (individual versus group, formal versus informal). However, effective R-mentoring arrangements tend toward certain known traits. All of which reduce to one word: friendship. R-mentoring stems from and fosters a camaraderie built over time for the purpose of benefiting from the perspective of someone very different from me. The subject matter of the friendship varies wildly among technical issues such as how to use a PDA (if you don't know what that stands for, get a reverse mentor immediately), or broader concerns such as why young people speak to each other in movie dialogue, or how church services are coming across to twentysomethings—or not coming across.

Most of my dozens of R-mentoring relationships developed out of "sacred accidents" and continue by informal means, most in-person but some via the Internet with friends I have never met face to face. To develop these ties, think of them as a new form of friendship (a skill we all possess) and simply approach a younger person you already know. Ask a few open and honest questions, to which you don't know the answer, without making speeches or commitments. If things go well, ask more questions, and let the relationship develop naturally. Experience in the business world indicates that mentoring bonds that feel mandatory or forced just about never work. Harvard Business School professor Monica Higgins summarizes the consensus of the business community: "Research suggests that a mentoring relationship works best when it evolves over time, in an informal fashion, through a shared interest in professional development. . . . Other research shows that effective mentoring relationships are those in which the communication styles of the mentor and the protégé match one another."[11]

Mutual enjoyment of the time together, and the flexibility to include elements outside the R-mentoring agenda, drive everything forward organically. In fact, seeking out a relationship purely on functional grounds eventually turns toxic, even if the younger person temporarily enjoys the high value placed on her or his opinion. A natural friendship works best.

Practicality

Reverse mentoring relationships may start by accident, but they thrive by design. Reverse mentoring offers one practical way to broaden my missional effectiveness by participating in the Kingdom out of my need rather than my surplus. Here are some key elements of being mentored by *Homo postmodernus*:

• *Check your attitude at the door.* A soft heart makes everything else work, while the need to appear knowledgeable and powerful pumps poison into the relationship. Remember, you are being crucified, not just educated. Your mentor will need some time to discern whether you ask questions because you're the *real deal* or just a *big deal* in your own mind. These interactions always surface the lust for the center that lurks inside us all, something my young friends will have to come to terms with themselves eventually. Given the chance, Mr. Miyagi will attempt to reassert himself. The R-mentoring setting offers a chance to deal him a nasty blow.

• *Ask questions, and then ask some more questions.* Your natural curiosity provides an enormous asset in the relationship. If you get stalled, ask your R-mentor to suggest some helpful topics; but that seldom proves necessary. If you resemble me, the list of things you do not get feels endless almost all the time, offering the opportunity to convert *obsolescence anxiety* (the encroaching fear of being useless) into the motivation to learn. What music are college students downloading (and why do they want to)? How will this affect congregational worship five years from now? Follow up your questions with even more questions that get at the details. You will be sorely tempted to give speeches using your R-mentor's statements as an opportunity to display what you know about the subject, or to parade even the faintest possibility that your GIQ is rising! Don't. I find this discipline difficult in the extreme, but also essential.

• *Take notes.* Recording valuable insights keeps the R-mentor motivated by displaying your seriousness and the value placed on his or her views. After all, you expect *them* to take notes on *your* talks.

• *Don't limit yourself to one person or format.* I use a variety of mentors (some older, some younger) depending on the subject at hand. Old-school mentoring insisted on one expert, but the Xbox world more likely requires rotating combinations that bring a lot more expertise to the table. Glen helps me with technology and the Internet, Joel advises me on art and culture, Kim and Heather share their poetry, Mark helps me understand ministry issues from a thirtysomething perspective, Adam coaches me on postmodernism without realizing it, Jordan is my Indy music guru, and so on. If things go really well, consider the possibility of a group R-mentoring experience, with your mentor selecting some peers to join in the exercise from time to time.

• *If it flops, let it go.* It's mentoring, not magic, so if the relationship just never develops the right chemistry, don't keep it alive by artificial means. Put this issue on the table right up front to avoid pain later. In truth, these relationships involve so much fun and so much discovery I do not understand why so few people seek them out.

- *Reciprocity: from protégé to partner.* Traditional mentoring centered on a fairly inflexible arrangement. Reverse mentoring opens up the possibility of a relationship in which both participants simultaneously teach and learn, each making the other an *adopted peer.* "As iron sharpens iron, so one man sharpens another."[12] Strictly one-way mentoring (upward or downward) resembles iron sharpening wood: all the power is on the side of the person whittling the other into his or her image. But with iron on both sides, each can be sharpened or conformed into the image of Christ through the work of the Spirit in the relationship.

A reciprocal relationship between young and old holds the potential for a missional partnership with the ethos of a family, in a way that no other method can produce. Paul's instructions for Timothy could become a reality: "Do not rebuke an older man harshly, but exhort him as if he were your father. Treat younger men as brothers, older women as mothers, and younger women as sisters, with absolute purity."[13] This passage seems to assume that the generations work together, a dynamic missing from many Christian ministries (and lives) today. The channels of communication opened by R-mentoring help the generations realize their mutual need for each other. As one market researcher puts it, "You can't rebel against helplessness."[14]

Teach Your Parents Well

The nine-year-old Xbox rookie awaits the opportunity to thrash me. No amount of training, even under Mr. Miyagi, offers the edge in skill or the margin of victory I lack. I am doomed. Do I possess the humility to accept instruction from a nine-year-old? Jesus said that things hidden from the wise have been revealed to "little children" and that entering the Kingdom requires becoming like them.[15] How many times have I missed the Kingdom because I insisted on being the adult in the relationship?

When Donnie, a youth pastor from Pennsylvania, tells me over coffee that bloggers in his youth group are migrating away from Xanga and toward Myspace (again, if these terms are unfamiliar to you, get a reverse mentor immediately), I face a choice: bluff by staying silent to give the appearance that I already know this, or admit I did not know it and start interviewing Donnie. Following the latter course teaches me things about youth that even their parents probably don't know and allow me to inquire into *why* this shift happens, and what it implies for life and mission on Planet iPod.

Over the same cup of coffee, I relate some experiences about how the book publishing business works to Donnie, an aspiring writer. Exchanging his youth research for my publishing experiences involves only a swapping of assets, a kind of trade. But admitting our mutual need makes us two dependent brothers in Christ who believe that our missional potential expands when we work in the kind of cooperation that denies giving the credit to any one person.

The business world realized the value of age diversity long ago. "Youth qualities by themselves are not enough," writes mentoring expert Matt Starcevich. "Experience, judgment and maturity are needed, too. Just talk to a refugee from one of the hundreds of dysfunctional dot coms. Of course the campus atmosphere was fun for a while, but after the first few management tantrums even the funkiest employees started muttering about the need for adult supervision."[16] So, if wisdom from experience offers stability, and wisdom from inexperience drives innovation, might not a combination be optimal for mission? I find it difficult to imagine a credible alternative.

On a recent blog I complained to my readers about people in airports overhearing my cell phone calls or talks with my wife and then choosing to intrude on the conversation to offer unsolicited help. Even though the issues involved tended toward the petty (are the good food places in this airport on *this* side of security or the *other* side?), I found these unwanted helpers completely annoying and sometimes told them so. Ventilating these sentiments online made me feel better.

Until I got the responses. Shocked and offended, my usually friendly readers rebuked my bad attitude, expressing dismay at such intolerance. That hurt. So I started thinking through why they (largely *Homo postmodernus*) saw things so differently, and I came to the conclusion that my home world enjoyed tidy categories such as public versus private along with the protocols of land-line telephones. The Xbox world, my readers taught me, discarded such notions long ago and regards helping a stranger in a public place not as an intrusion but as the polite and ethical thing to do. After all, by holding a conversation in a public place, I intruded on them *first*. So I blogged again, this time with the title, "I Was Wrong."

A group of R-mentors, many of whom I have never met, taught me that their assumptions did not match mine, and that when using a cell phone I was on their cultural turf. What would happen to our ministries if an experience like this were repeated in each of them? Realizing that reaching out to people means meeting them on their turf, could we humble ourselves to learn their assumptions, for the purpose of loving them more unconditionally and communicating with them more effectively? The answer is only found off road.

Chapter Five

Witness

The Discipline of Spiritual Friendship

The ride from the airport to the university took us through exotic mountainous terrain guarded by redwood trees and camouflaged by mist. Four of us negotiated the turns and switchbacks of the route, strapped to minivan seats and accompanied by thousands of other drivers all going mountain climbing in their SUVs and second-hand commuter cars. Inside our van, the scenery also held surprises. Justin (the driver) and Rusty (seated behind Justin) had picked up Louis, a hitchhiker, who needed a ride to another university, intending to engage in a spiritual conversation with him. The hitchhiker method of evangelism, common in my youth, now held only nostalgia; surely no one thought seriously of using this old school technique for securing a captive audience. Plus, picking up a stranger seemed like a good way to end up on *America's Most Wanted*—as the victim. ("Seminary Professor Slain by Student Serial Killer," the headline would announce.) Rusty and Justin seemed immune to such middle-aged paranoia. They simply saw an opportunity to dialogue with a new friend about spiritual issues and took it. The shortest distance between two points of view is straight talk.

Louis shattered all my hitchhiker stereotypes. In fact, he borrowed rides only because he lived and worked in another part of the state and found sharing someone else's car the only sensible way to maintain his multisite lifestyle. He proved extremely bright and tirelessly articulate. He was also a film major. This last attribute caught our attention and began an hour-long discussion on the nature of his favorite genre (documentary) and his preferred mode of artistic expression in film (editing). We had a number of favorite filmmakers in common, including Alfred Hitchcock, and explored topics ranging from Foucault's claim that our lives merely transfer us from one "prison" to another to the value of documentaries as carriers of "truth."

When I asked Louis what kind of film depicts the "most truth," he replied "documentaries that have no words, no narrator, where they just show you truth with the images." He claimed that narrated films leave audiences thinking "good documentary!" but image-only documentaries move audiences to act on what they see. For Louis, truth is best served raw. Turning a corner, I confessed that as a Christian preacher I often wonder how my version of truth plays in the minds of audiences. The word *preacher* itself connotes a top-down approach to communicating, with the speaker in the authoritative position and the listener bound to hear and obey. Louis agreed, citing church architecture as proof: one person stands in an elevated pulpit and talks down to the masses sitting obediently in parallel rows below. He interpreted this format as itself a statement about power relationships, one he found anathema.

So I asked him how he recommended that Christians change their communication style to make the message comprehensible to those investigating the faith. His advice centered on a novel idea: "Make everyone a preacher." In other words, Louis's spiritual interests drew him only toward communication arenas featuring an almost purely participatory format. In fact, he cited a friend who recently walked him through a series of dialogues about the Bible, which awakened in him a living faith in the Christian God. Drawing others into discussion and even debate about the nature and function of the faith seemed to Louis the only way to communicate with people these days. As our trip neared its end, I expressed regret that the schedule for my talks at the Christian university afforded no opportunity for him to attend and give me some critique. Silently I wished I could speak at *his* university (famous as a bastion of postmodernism). As Louis stepped out of the minivan for the final trek to his dorm, I realized this film major taught me more about communication in an hour than some whole courses on the subject.

This chapter defines relationship with people I will call the sought, people like Louis, as an off-road spiritual discipline essential to the kind of personal transformation that can make evangelism something we live rather than just a message we say. Jesus spent thirty years in relationship with people of all kinds before beginning his three-year public ministry, a ratio of ten to one. No wonder the common people heard him gladly; he spoke their language, knew their stories, and felt their pain. Relationship involves more than learning about others as a form of market research so we can adjust our methods to their sensibilities. It also involves internal change catalyzed by spending time with the people God reaches out to through us, people who need a completely new kind of life but who lack the ability to acquire it on their own. This sort of life comes only from the God who loves them.

Mental Models of the Sought

Healthy relationship requires that we think and speak about each other in life-giving ways. Knowing how to do this when you're speaking with those who practice other spiritualities is a daunting challenge. After a public interfaith discussion in Boston, for example, a pastor friend told me that some audience members reacted very strongly to his use of terms such as *non-Christian* and *unbeliever*. The words carried us-versus-them overtones that blocked the Christian message for those who felt they were being cast as spiritually inferior outsiders, as unpeople. Though anyone who takes Scripture seriously need not back away from its characterization of the lost, how we frame this issue profoundly influences our relationship with the sought.

Jesus compared them to a "lost sheep," a "lost coin," and a "lost" son.[1] However, the common feature of his parables about lost people centers on the fact that someone recovered the sheep, the coin, or the son, someone who cared deeply. The good shepherd leaves the ninety-nine to search for the one sheep. A desperate woman sweeps and cleans her entire home to locate one of her ten precious coins. Even a rebellious son returning home and offering to live as a slave receives the welcome of a king from his father. For Jesus, the waywardness of the person in each parable establishes the opportunity for recovery and redemption, a portrait of his own mission: "For the Son of Man came to seek and to save what was lost."[2] Using this backdrop, I suggest that we might refer to lost people not as seekers but as the sought. The assumption is that God through Christ is the ultimate Seeker, caring infinitely more about them than we imagine, and seeking those He loves in the sacrificial form of Jesus' death and the triumphant terms of His resurrection.

This simple change in terminology hardly represents a comprehensive theology of salvation, but it reflects God's heart for people in a way that recognizes their lostness, their need for the Seeker who makes saving grace available through the death and resurrection of Jesus, while emphasizing God's initiative as the heartbeat of mission. It also exposes the danger of keeping two sets of books (lexicons, actually). One consists of the very direct, theologically derived terms evangelicals use within our subculture to discuss the status of the lost ("pagan," "sinner"). The other involves the softer, market-savvy words we craft to minimize negative reaction when interacting with other spiritual cultures ("seeker," "pre-Christian"). Among the users of the latter lexicon, I sometimes sense the embarrassment awaiting them if their insider language ever becomes known among friends and family outside the subculture. This inconsistency speaks to our own discomfort over the issue of how to refer to the lost. In one survey, 56 percent of the unchurched found the term lost offensive, with only a tiny fraction reporting favorable feelings about a church that described them this way. The two most acceptable terms of the seven tested in this study were *inquirer* and *explorer*. Even the term seeker found approval among only 40 percent, and that disproportionately among Midwesterners.[3] Adding "the sought" as a descriptor offers one way forward out of this dilemma by placing emphasis on God's mission in Christ on a wayward planet. A missional person, then, cultivates "Seeker-sensitivity" by staying attuned and cooperative with God's efforts to reach the sought by expressing the power of Christ's death and resurrection through the Church in its many forms.

The words used to describe anyone's spiritual condition (always a tricky proposition) never come from a vacuum; they flow out of our hearts, out of our theological assumptions and personal prejudices. Several mental models of the sought, usually unspoken, lead to the toxic relationships that make faith seem poisonous to them while blocking our own path to transformation, the path of feeling God's heart for the world. However, the issue here involves much more than just wording; it forces the larger question of "Who are the sought to us?" Some of the available mental models of viewing the sought make clear why a missional life eludes so many.[4]

"Souls with Ears"

An antiquated (thankfully) missionary expression, the phrase "souls with ears" casts people as disembodied spirits mainly in need of pardon for the sin that separates them from God and dooms them for eternity. From this perspective, God's Kingdom almost exclusively concerns His rule over their eternal destiny, with little regard for other aspects of life, encouraging the Church to focus on mission in the same way. Thus the task centers on firing "gospel bullets" (the content of the message) at the target audience until their resistance collapses and they join our cause. The evangelistic efforts of sincere Christians flirt with this mental model as they reduce the gospel to mere ideas deserving assent and shrink complicated human beings to invisible spirits, radically deemphasizing other aspects of God's mission such as compassion and justice. I cringe, for example, to recall the sermons preached in the wake of September 11, 2001, framing this catastrophe as a welcome chance for America to repent, a viewpoint that was lost on those whose loved ones were torn from them that day.[5] Similarly, counting "decision" cards collected at the end of an Easter musical and announcing the number of "souls" won represents a legitimate aspiration, but it risks sending the same message that people are units of spirituality we can count like the offering, with the after-life being our only concern.

"Barbarians to Civilize"

The barbarian model, at the other end of the spectrum, views people outside the Church as almost another race of beings. In other words, instead of disembodied spirits needing only deliverance from eternal damnation, these strangers represent soulless primitives requiring civilization. Their issue revolves not just around eternity but around replacing their traits with those of Christian insiders for whom "salvation" seems to include looking and acting like a Christian insider. This look-and-feel theology makes the Kingdom of God almost synonymous with the imposition of my culture on yours, making you an enemy who must be overcome. This mental model shows up, along with small crowds of protestors, at Christian conventions carrying signs that say things like "God Hates Fags." Or in the sermons that I heard (or heard of) that interpreted the tsunami of 2004 as God's judgment on Muslims for terrorism, or Hurricane Katrina in 2005 as his wrath poured out on vice in New Orleans. Clearly, this model risks every conceivable form of imperialism, from cultural cloning (forcing a rain forest tribe into Western garb) to colonization (treating a "reached" group as existing to serve the interests of the "sending" group) to outright conquest in the name of Christ, all of which share an ugly place in the history of missions.

"Invisible People"

Not every mental model even acknowledges the existence of the sought. Some Christian insiders simply never see people in spiritual terms, living as if they operated cash registers, typed at computers, or poured coffee but never caught God's eye. Reaching out in love never gets on our agenda if we view God's concern as revolving around me and those like me, the citizens of Christendom, a sort of gated community that offers no real protection for its residents but effectively keeps nonmembers out, making them undetectable, stealth people. God's mission in the world then devolves into taking care of the visible—maintaining our institutions (mowing the grass of the gated community) and polishing our own righteousness, like the Pharisees who loved the best seats in the synagogues and made lengthy prayers but also devoured the houses of widows. A gated community exists for only one reason: to send the message that we live on the inside, and you do not.

The temptation to view people as disembodied spirits or objects of conquest places God's mission in constant jeopardy, but I suspect that simple invisibility poses a larger problem. The religious authorities of His day challenged Jesus repeatedly for associating with people who by all rights should have remained invisible, on the margins of decent society: "This man welcomes sinners and eats with them," they whined.[6] Yet for all the attention garnered by these outbursts against those viewed as unworthy of God's love, the quieter habit of dissolving lost sheep into the social background serves just as effectively, and probably more frequently, to neutralize our participation in God's mission. Read through the lens of Jesus' parables: we seldom beat travelers and leave them to die in a ditch, but we often pass by on the other side with ease.

These mental models warp our view of the very people Jesus sends us to love and reach, making them ethereal spirits, dangerous enemies, or nothing at all. Jesus did not die for caricatures; He died for human beings. When we act as if the potential recipients of Christ's sacrifice represent some alien race of invaders from outer space, we violate Paul's command to "be wise in the way you act toward outsiders; make the most of every opportunity."[7] Our terminology and behavior easily reflect a distinct lack of wisdom in exactly these relationships, even for those attempting to write books about the subject. How can something as expansive as God's love for people end up trapped and warped within the confines of our own distorted perspective?

"You Seem So Busy"

In a coffee house for lunch with a pastor and a subsequent meeting with a friend, I noticed Bob, an owner of the establishment, working behind the counter taking orders. When I first started frequenting his establishment during my days as a pastor in the community, I enjoyed talking with Bob several times each week. We started with typical customer service chatter but soon moved on to the struggles of running a business in our downtown district, the issues of overwork that we both faced, and a growing list of other mutual concerns. I liked him, and I think he found it intriguing to develop a relationship with a pastor, perhaps his first. As our friendship grew over several years, we spoke of spiritual matters more than once.

Then my life and my job changed, placing me in an office or on the road, or just generally with Christians almost all the time. No amount of guilt, confession, or hand-wringing ever seemed to cure this condition. Perhaps it goes with the territory of the parachurch professional (or perhaps I just like the convenience of this rationalization). But Bob's life changed too. He opened some new locations for his business and began spending some time at them. Somehow, a couple years passed without our talking or even seeing each other.

Then one day I walked up to the counter at the coffeehouse with a friend to order the soup and sandwich special for lunch, and there was Bob. A little nervous at first, we played eye tag for a moment or so, neither of us sure where our relationship stood, and neither wanting to presume on the other. Then, our eye contact trajectories finally crossed for the appropriate number of seconds and we said "Hello." It seemed right, as if no time had passed at all. We both felt the grace of each other's silent forgiveness for failing to keep in touch.

Later, Bob brought our sandwiches to the table personally— very unusual, given the full-house lunch business he now enjoyed. So I started talking to him, inquiring about the success of the new locations and expressing regret for not having spoken to him for so long. I also assured Bob that his coffeehouse was still "home." He replied that, seeing me a few times recently, he wanted to stop by for a chat, "but you seem so busy."

Those five words cut me. My friends kept talking, but I only pretended to hear what they said for the next minute or so. Then I regained my composure and pretended to be OK until I moved on to my next meeting—with a Christian.

Several factors brought me to this position of almost total disconnection from Bob.

Vision Drift

The almost exclusively Christian relationships in my life at that time exerted a silent influence on my sense of mission, slowly morphing it into a sly counterfeit in which my service to the Church somehow discharged my obligation to live a personal witness of Christ. The passion for seeing the sought meet the Seeker ignited in me by the Pentecostal/Charismatic revivals of the mid-1990s cooled into something more like an affection for the *idea* of mission. Bill Easum warns of this danger when he writes: "Vision is often determined by who you spend most of your time with. Consider Paul's call to the Gentiles in Asia Minor. Paul was in Antioch working among Gentiles when he had the vision of the man asking him to come over to Macedonia. So the question might be for some of us, with whom are we spending most of our time? If it is among church people, then our vision is focused on them. If it is among the unwashed, non-Christian, pagan gentiles, it is most likely for them."[8]

I love the Church. I love God's people. But spending all of my time among them carried the penalty of desensitizing me to the needs of the sought, making them invisible. I wonder now how many times I passed Bob on the street or in the mall without ever seeing him.

Ministry Drift

If Bob is any indication, the sought see me as unapproachably busy, making the ministry itself something that blocks our relationship rather than building it. I recall one small rural subdivision, for example, in which the neighbors knew us as "the people who are gone all the time." In another, more suburban development, the couple living next door saw me returning from a trip and made a point of telling my wife that they only now believed she was actually married. Previously, they assumed her references to a husband represented a security measure at best and a mystery at worst, since they possessed no independent evidence of my existence.

In this same way, ministry activity (or work, or recreation, or travel) masquerades easily as missional activity, creating the paradox of the "overchurched underachiever." As New Testament commentator William Barclay writes, "In the world and in the church we are constantly in peril of loving systems more than we love God and more than we love men."[9] What I love expresses itself in what I do. Skipping many trips to the coffee house and obsessing on work while there told Bob that I lacked the kind of love it takes to see him, a failure plain to Bob but not obvious to me at all. His friendly comment revealed that I now treated ministry as an end in addition to a means, an attitude that reduced the sought to phantoms, ghostly outlines not worthy of my attention. Only love paints those people so I see them in vivid, three-dimensional detail, calling my eye and then my life to them.

Schedule Drift

Without realizing it, I assumed that the early part of my friendship with Bob, involving many visits to the coffee house and many conversations, served as a permanent template. It never occurred to me that, as midlife professionals, both of us would experience lots of changes in our jobs. When those changes happened (he grew his business, and I switched from parish to parachurch work), no plan B materialized to sustain the relationship. We lacked a fallback position, a way of keeping in touch once the spontaneous phase of the friendship became a casualty of our new scheduling realities. As a person wanting to be Seeker-sensitive, this obligation falls to me.

This simple practical error made Bob just as invisible as any form of isolation or failure of love. The coffee house represented our only shared social space, and the absence of a plan to place me there on a predictable basis erased Bob from my life just as certainly as one of us moving out of town. The inability to adjust to changes, adapting the relationship to new circumstances, almost guarantees a breakdown at some point. Though I play only a small part in the many ways God seeks out friends like Bob, I owe both the Seeker and the sought better than this.

All of these dynamics conspire to put the sought into stealth mode, making them an afterthought at best and causing them to disappear altogether at worst. The Seeker never forgets them, but the Church often lacks the grace to keep its spiritual eyes open for the presence of God among those He seeks out in Christ. Writer Kathleen Norris comments on the prevalence of God's efforts in her own life as she reflects on her book *The Virgin of Bennington*: "I really think this book shows where a religious conversion comes from. It doesn't come out of a vacuum, but it might come out of a very messy life. Out of someone who really isn't even aware that God is working in the world, and certainly in her life. But I think that as I wrote the book I was very conscious that God was really present and active all along. It's just that I was too dumb to notice it."[10]

Although direct awareness of God's activity escapes the sought at times, the Church needs to embrace relationship with them in faith that no one lives a life outside of God's influence and that, given time, the Seeker will make Himself known in ways that invite the sought into a new relationship and a new kind of life. Our friendship certainly influences the sought, but God also uses these relationships to change our hearts.

N2

I wait for a plane at the N2 gate of the Seatac (Seattle-Tacoma) airport, reading a book and thinking about what I need to write in my next e-mail newsletter. Across the narrow aisle from me a thirtyish man sits on a veined, black vinyl chair just like mine. But his situation couldn't be more different. Drawing two children close, he speaks to them in hushed, earnest tones with the kind of inflection people use for matters of extreme gravity. The man uses adult words like *closure* in his monologue with a girl and boy who both look somewhere around seven years old.

Because I'm just four feet away, I overhear the man explaining in a roundabout way to these two squirmy youngsters why they will never see their sibling again. Kurt is dead. At first I am angry: Why on earth would this young father explain a child's death at gate N2 instead of at home in private? A small wave of compassion whispers that he probably has no choice; who would have this conversation at gate N2 given any other option? As the conversation gets more and more intense and detailed, I grow more and more embarrassed, wishing I could close my ears, temporarily putting them on mute.

The man's eyes are red, as he sends the silent children off to the newsstand, carefully coaching them to stay within an arm's length of each other, perhaps fearing even more separations. The break gives him the chance to place a cell phone call in that too-loud voice that we all use—which only makes things worse for me. Now he pours his heart out to someone on the other end, venting anger and confusion about the gash in his heart, saying things too painful for children (or seminary professors) to overhear. However, he seems to have no problem with me overhearing. I'm wishing I was one of the kids just now, off at the newsstand.

My attention returns to the book I am reading, Doug Pagitt's *Preaching Reimagined,* in which he makes the case for a participatory model of sermon preparation and distribution (not "delivery," which is the wrong word). This book caught my interest because of my own background in communication and a recent assignment to teach preaching for my seminary. I enjoyed the book but found myself resisting his case for replacing "speaching" (remarkably similar to our hitchhiker Louis's depiction of preaching) with "progressional dialogue" (in which both the sought and the already-found collaborate to explore the implications of the sacred text). I wrote many critical comments in the oversized margins and rebutted his claims mentally at every turn. The preaching in the book of Acts failed to meet any definition of participatory dialogue in my mind.

That is, I pushed back until I experienced the stereo sensation of reading the end of chapter eight while simultaneously overhearing the young father's anguish at N2. The concluding paragraph reads: "I can't imagine Jenell [a bereaved mother], or anyone else, having to sit through a generic sermon on God's faithfulness offered by someone more concerned about the church agenda than the real experience of the people listening. I can't imagine any preacher arrogant enough to presume to know how Jenell and her husband should live in light of their grief and pain."[11]

In isolation, my arguments against Doug's preaching model probably sounded like this:

- Sure, but that only works with a relatively tiny group of artsy cultural creatives living in midtown lofts.
- The Holy Spirit can make preaching specific to any individual.
- Dialogue is just another monolithic method in a world of multiple learning styles.

But hearing the pain of the young father's ruined heart leaking out through his words put these very conventional complaints aside, and I started asking the hard questions of myself.

If the sad and angry father's seat were a church pew rather than a plastic chair at N2, how would the typical sermon speak to him about the Seeker who is no stranger to pain? My messages on the mission of the Church, or the power of God, or the importance of relationship might represent only the irrelevance of the Christian community, the negligence of a God who failed him, highlighting the value of something he had already lost forever. But then I think, "When do I listen to his voice?" When do I love him enough to discover his issues, to create an opportunity for him to meet the Seeker in the text in some unexpected way? The synergy of Doug's perspective and this real world crisis opened up my thinking about how preaching needs to work. In the presence of the Seeker, somehow this young man's unbearable pain penetrated my defenses to become a gift, the gift of transformation. My few moments as the man across the aisle from him changed things. Perhaps no texts on preaching (or anything else) ought to be written without consulting the sought.

Sacred Coffee

Despite the current vogue of criticizing PowerPoint, I have to admit that this software was responsible for beginning my relationship with Bob. When I was handed the check that bought our congregation's first video projector, I knew some big changes lay ahead. Armed with my first laptop and the knowledge that my thoughts could now be digitized and projected using PowerPoint, I headed to Bob's coffee house to work on my sermons with a new zeal. The caffeine helped, and I found that the isolation from the blur of the office functioned as a secondary stimulant. PowerPoint felt like a new toy as I began transferring what had been hardcopy sermon outlines into slides that I hoped, with the help of a little clip art (very hip in the 1990s), to parlay into a big response. The coffee house grew into my second office a day or two each week, serving as the site for staff meetings, counseling, and virtually every other pastoral function. But my sermons remained conventional, using projected slides to create what amounted to an electric blackboard from which I lectured.

Sitting over a two-dollar bottomless cup of coffee and a glowing laptop screen for many hours connected me regularly with Bob and his co-owner Ryan. Although they never asked me about my sermons, I began to ask myself some things. Looking down at my screen and then looking up at Bob and Ryan, I wondered about their reaction to the thoughts I composed there every week. I concluded that, even projected on a screen (a novelty to our church at the time) my talks meant forty-five minutes of Seinfeldian "yada,

yada, yada" to them, since the talks assumed the logic and language of church insiders framed in a contemporary, conversational style.

Over time, drinking coffee and writing sermons in the presence of the sought cultivated changes in my approach without ever involving a conscious decision. The length of my talks dropped by a third, concepts and vocabulary grew simpler, and text on slides gave way to images or nothing at all. The change came to my attention when a few church insiders complained that the talks now lacked the depth and complexity they expected on Sunday morning. But it was too late. A return to churchy content and style, effectively disenfranchising the sought, held no attraction—especially once we saw a positive response from them (and from the vast majority of the congregation), realizing along the way that it was possible as well as necessary to speak to both groups simultaneously.

I blame Bob and Ryan. Under the influence of their friendship, drinking coffee with the sought became almost sacramental, convincing me that sermons should be composed only among them. As Pagitt puts it, "Listening to the voices of others is an essential part of being the church. We were never meant to close in on ourselves."[12] If our words are not composed among the sought, why should we expect them to listen when those words are delivered? Their friendship holds the power to transform us, if we set aside our mental models and begin to see them not as enemies but as common friends of the Seeker.

Chapter Six

Humility

The Discipline of Decreasing

My commute to work takes about half an hour. The round trip traps me in my car for an hour each working day, facing a grim choice: risk not hearing a siren by piping music directly into my brain from an iPod, or risk losing my brain by listening to most local radio. For a while, NPR offered a refuge from this dilemma, until I stumbled one day across a familiar voice on an FM station, the voice of a onetime televangelist now largely exiled to radio in the South. A passing sample of his program (he owns the station) slowly grew into a regular pattern of listening during virtually every commute. Despite my wife's protestations (because I arrived home angry), my habit grew into a fascination that needed feeding every drive time. The familiar voice became a preset button on my car radio, a real place of honor in a broadcast market offering a station on every available frequency.

This man's programs made me angry because I believe that the style and content of this broadcast turned off so many people to the good news about Jesus that it essentially canceled all of our own efforts. (I took to calling people like this "erasers" because they wipe away anything we accomplish with our own lives.) In fact, when listening I often recalled the campus pastor who told me that the atheists club at his university gathered regularly to watch certain high-profile Christian television programs—for entertainment. They found mockery great fun. I imagined this same dynamic operating whenever the familiar voice took the air, moving cynical secularists to turn the radio up and fragile seekers to turn off the radio—and perhaps the gospel. The thought of my own ministry canceled out every day by this kind of antievangelism almost brought me to despair at times.

The angry reaction passed eventually, but the fascination did not. I kept on listening. Perplexed by my own behavior, I asked Larry, the regional official in my denomination whom we will meet in Chapter Eight, what he thought it all meant. "You're trying to understand fundamentalism," he replied. Yes. My listening habits arose not from a warped obsession with formerly famous preachers but out of the same curiosity, the hunger to understand, that propelled me into field research in the American Church in the first place. Every broadcast represented an EKG of the fundamentalist mind, a readout on how the world looks from that perspective and why this viewpoint compels allegiance from so many people at the same time it has the opposite effect on so many others. The broadcast served as the natural counterpoint to my years of walking with the younger leaders of the experimental church, allowing me to listen in on the body of Christ—in stereo.

Months of broadcasts revealed a common thread: I am right, and everyone else is wrong. The familiar voice and his staff never said so outright but implied it with their nonstop criticism of every form of Christianity even faintly distinct from their own Southern, hyperconservative, Pentecostal variety. The list of enemies of the faith included seeker-sensitive churches, Christian psychology, Rick Warren, addiction recovery groups, prosperity teaching, G-12 small groups, and countless other forms of the faith, especially those found in the conservative evangelical subculture. The familiar voice practiced a new brand of apologetics, one aimed at defending his own narrow interpretation of the gospel against competition from *within* the Christian community. Presumably other faiths, other issues, or even other forms of Christianity outside evangelicalism involved error so profound and so self-evident as not to merit much airtime. The threat came from within, from those posing as the real thing.

These conclusions seemed to rest on an unspoken assumption inherent in every program: I have the right to tell you what is truth and what is error. This breathtaking premise found reinforcement

in one form or another in virtually every sermon, interview, or discussion featured on the broadcast. Beware of seeker churches; they
do not preach the gospel. Beware of cell groups; they do not foster
dependence on God. Beware of anything purpose-driven; Rick
Warren might approve of it. And so forth. Each warning carried
the implication that the familiar voice somehow merited the position of arbiter of truth, his voice deserving to be the loudest, with
his role justifiably central to a Church trying to find its way.

This chapter makes a case for humility as an off-road spiritual
discipline critical to the missional life. Unlike my radio fundamentalist, whose voice demands a hearing, a central role, exclusive loy-
alty to one narrow perspective on a two-thousand-year-old faith
practiced in innumerable forms among millions of people, humility
is exemplified by the words of John the Baptist about the meaning
of preparing the way for Christ: "He must become greater; I must
become less."[1] Humility is the discipline of decreasing the scale of
my own story until it fits inside the Jesus story, until he defines me
rather than my defining him, until Paul's words become reality: "For
you died, and your life is now hidden with Christ in God."[2] Mission
without humility tends to make my autobiography seem like the
story of the whole world (at least to me), producing self-centered
extremism. Humility without mission disconnects my autobiography from a strong sense of purpose, producing self-preserving futility. Humility and mission do sometimes find each other, as they did
in John when he acknowledges a subservient role that points to the
greater role of the Christ for whom he prepared the way.

"I Am Not the Christ": Negative Humility

Traveling speakers tell a lot of the same jokes. For years, many of
them have warmed up crowds by referring to "my latest book" as
Perfect Humility and How I Attained It. People laugh for a reason:
others observe humility in us, but proclaiming it ourselves defines its
absence conclusively. Escaping this conundrum (developing a trait
I'm not allowed to realize I have) requires thinking about humility

as possessing both a positive and a negative valence. The positive valence involves specific kinds of behavior in the real world, while the negative ensures that, like John, I know who and what I am not.

John shared much with Jesus, including some genetic material (as Jesus' cousin), profound experiences with the Holy Spirit, prophetic insight, proclamation of the Kingdom's nearness, a message of repentance, a gift for annoying those in power, an arrest, and a tragic death. John's influence profoundly affected Palestine and other parts of the Mediterranean basin; his disciples were present among the Jewish communities of the empire's other provinces.[3]

Having this sort of influence could tempt one to regard oneself as living the big story, the ultimate autobiography, deserving the position of truth arbiter.

But John's life loses its meaning unless he divorces himself from this central role reserved only for the Son of God. John breaks free from the pull of the center with the negative statement, "He did not fail to confess, but confessed freely, 'I am not the Christ.'" The multitudes pressed him (as they sometimes press us today) to take the central role: "They asked him, 'Then who are you? Are you Elijah?' He said, 'I am not.' 'Are you the Prophet?' He answered, 'No.'"[4] His denials are reminiscent of Peter's reply in Acts 10 to an adoring Cornelius, who had fallen at the Christian preacher's feet in reverence. "'Stand up,' he said, 'I am only a man myself.'"[5] Paul and Barnabas experienced the same challenge in the city of Lystra, when the citizens proclaimed their divinity in the wake of a miraculous healing. Despite their protestations, the populace barely restrained themselves from offering sacrifice.[6] The pressure to make my story the defining one comes from both internal and external sources. If I fail to convince myself, the crowd may convince me—how else do I account for their presence? John escaped this temptation with one word: *no*.

This word sounds simple, but summoning the motivation to say it means thinking about humility as more complex than a little self-deprecating humor (the most common counterfeit among leaders) or an "aw shucks" sense of mild embarrassment when receiving a compliment (more a symptom of low self-esteem than a fruit of the

Spirit). These superficial traits tend to be substitutes for the work of grace required to decrease me until only the Jesus story matters, the same way Jesus decreased himself until only his redemptive purpose mattered. Several negative statements are useful in opening my heart to this work of grace by the Spirit.

I Am Not Omniscient

God resists the proud. Not needing this kind of resistance, I opened a talk before several hundred youth pastors in Texas with a confession of my abject lack of experience in their ministry genre (apart from one sermon preached to a youth group with limited success). This announcement invoked a moment of uncomfortable silence, shocking their profoundly pragmatic sensibilities, followed by that "What's *this* guy doing here?" look that proved impossible to conceal even in a large room. But the simple admission of the truth filled me with a sense of liberty to communicate without anxiety, something I seldom experience. I spent part of the talk, for example, naming the things they all feared to say to their senior pastors (since I have been one). There is so much less to remember when I don't know much, and so much less pressure if I don't feel the need to know more than every other person in the room. My ignorance-based talk ended about an hour later with the only standing ovation I've ever received. Perhaps our problems revolve not so much around knowing too little as around the perception that we know so much. Omniscience involves too great a burden for us to carry. Ignorance befriends me by offering a daily opportunity to learn who I am not. Under extreme duress, John questioned the fullness of Jesus' identity but never attempted to expand in ways that infringed on the role reserved for Christ alone.[7]

I Am Not Omnipotent

People with a high sense of felt power (the perception, true or false, that their influence is very significant) tend not to hide it in conversation, a trait painfully obvious to others but apparently unknown to them. They may openly revel in individual competence or in their organizational position, claiming to trust God for the utterly impossible, but quietly regarding everything else as their domain. A minister acquaintance, for example, walked up to me at a retreat, shook my hand, and began a typical binge-and-purge conversation. While we shook hands, he immediately launched into a five-minute monologue about a piece of news he wanted to tell me (that's the binge part, bingeing on my attention) and then segued seamlessly into a field report about some recent preaching adventures (that's the purge part). I counted the seconds, silently pleading for this personal infomercial to end, allowing me the opportunity to withdraw graciously and my tormenter a chance to stalk his next audience.

High felt-power people thrive on the prospect of parading their competence before peers—or anyone else who will listen. Sometimes we even corrupt an otherwise valid kind of witness by calling these one-person-shows "testimonies." Power is the opiate of the faithful. Truth is the antidote. Get a high felt-power individual into an arena that renders competence irrelevant (be it a video game or a cross-cultural experience) and watch the person melt down. In fact, I thought writing this paragraph carried a small measure of payback for enduring so many monologues, until the exercise forced me to realize that I often fall into the same trap. John resisted the temptation of power in part by not performing any miraculous signs, avoiding even the possibility of confusing his story with that of the Christ.[8]

I Am Not Omnipresent

Our calendars function as lie detectors. If I assert falsely that my life reflects balance, rest, and peace, my schedule calls me a liar to my face because I want to be all things to all people—*all at the same time*. The seductive notion that every meeting, every need, every relationship legitimately requires my constant presence perpetuates the feeling of indispensability. The urgent sense that the fate of civilization hangs on getting to the next event signifies a lust for omnipresence that artificially inflates my story at the expense of the

Jesus story. The allure of personal significance grows every time the alarm goes off in my PDA, playing a tiny hymn to my importance.

Moses and Solomon, however, took another, entirely opposite approach. Assuming the throne of Israel, Solomon confessed, "I am only a little child and do not know how to carry out my duties." Moses, facing the enervating prospect of ruling on thousands of individual issues brought to him by the Israelites in the wilderness, received a warning from his father-in-law Jethro: "The work is too heavy for you; you cannot handle it alone."[9] If leaders of this stature hit the limits of their ability to connect with everyone, then our own adrenalin-driven rush for omnipresence reveals itself as pointless. Even though John's disciples extended his influence around Palestine (and ultimately the other Roman provinces), he rejoiced to hear from them of Jesus that "everyone is going to him," preferring to close out his role as forerunner rather than compete for market share with the one for whom he opened the way.

Negative humility acknowledges the absence of divine attributes and embraces this void as an opportunity for God's grace to operate unimpaired by my self-serving intentions. The tendency to grow my story at God's expense seems so natural to me that I can be inoculated against the awareness of this danger most days. Increasing my role and decreasing God's feels so normal that otherwise legitimate vocabulary sometimes mutates to describe it. Terms such as *professional*, *commitment*, *strategy*, and *multitasking* may seem to define commendable traits, but they may also serve as code words, disguising a heart attitude that says, "God is very big, but so am I." A Jungian therapist might refer to this malady as "inflation." I call it sin. To counteract this tendency, we need vocabulary that gives the off-road grace of humility a better chance to survive.

"Sent Ahead of Him": Positive Humility

John's negative statement of his identity represented only a partial picture of his ministry. He also asserted a specific, positive sense of the mission for which God sent him: "I am not the Christ *but am sent ahead of him*."[10] John describes Jesus as the bridegroom to whom the bride (his followers) belonged, making his own role that of "the friend who attends the bridegroom" who "is full of joy when he hears the bridegroom's voice."[11] John knew his mission exactly and articulated it in detail. We too can express attitudes and practices that help to clear the space for the growth of humility as a behavior rather than just a demeanor.

"I Don't Know"

In the information age, the list of things I do not know grows every second. My knowledge creeps forward like a glacier on my best day while the stock of available data accumulates like an avalanche rolling downhill. Trying to base decisions on all of this hard information sounds both logical and practical but often involves as much guesswork as anything else. As even leading decision-making theorists concede, "Whenever uncertainty exists, there can be no guarantee that a smart choice will lead to good consequences."[12] When I add to this the fact that we do not know what conditions will confront us tomorrow, what is truly in the hearts of those we will encounter, or even how we should pray about these things,[13] the notion that information automatically equals control becomes absurd.

The real problem begins, however, when I face the choice of saying that my knowledge is limited. My natural longing to want to appear more knowledgeable than I am asserts itself at the slightest provocation. On countless occasions, for example, friends ask what I think of this or that book, assuming that most of the Library of Congress has found its way to my house. After stammering for a moment (during which I mentally shop reply options, searching for one that tells the truth without making me look too bad), I admit that I bought the book but am too busy writing to have read it. The mild shock and disappointment that usually follows embarrasses me and sometimes lowers my stock in the inquisitor's opinion, especially if the person depends on me to know all of the literature at the front edge of thinking on the Church (an impossible feat for anyone, but an impression that part of me wants others to have). The only safety is in the truth.

The benefits of telling the truth, of saying "I don't know," manifest themselves in quite specific ways. An admission of ignorance keeps me accountable to others while preventing me from becoming a gifted fake, bluffing my way through one encounter after another, allowing people to believe a fabricated version of what I am by silence and subtle misdirection. I find unbearable the idea that I might indirectly coach a younger person to emulate the delicate arts of clever wording and tactical omission that allow others to believe us to be more than we are. This fear alone is enough to force the truth into the open by giving it specific vocabulary.

"I don't know" is a positive statement about my identity as a person of limited knowledge, putting into behavioral terms the recognition that I am not omniscient. Until I say it, until I confess it, humility remains a theory and not a life lived in God. The more I say it, the more truth I tell, the more the Spirit can cultivate spiritual fruit within me.

"I'm Sorry"

When warning the early Church about the dangers of harming each other with the spoken word, James comments that "we all stumble in many ways."[14] Each of our lives serves as Exhibit A for the case James makes to his readers. Our natural longing to exert personal power moves us to use it on others, sometimes deliberately and sometimes inadvertently, but always painfully. The closer the relationship, the more my ersatz omnipotence stings the person or group on which I choose to exercise it. Strangely, the properties of love actually create the conditions under which the damage is most devastating. C. S. Lewis describes the irony:

> To love at all is to be vulnerable. Love anything, and your heart will certainly be wrung and possibly be broken. If you want to make sure

of keeping it intact, you must give your heart to no one, not even to an animal. Wrap it carefully round with hobbies and little luxuries; avoid all entanglements; lock it up safe in the casket or coffin of your selfishness. But in that casket—safe, dark, motionless, airless—it will change. It will not be broken; it will become unbreakable, impenetrable, irredeemable. . . . The only place outside Heaven where you can be perfectly safe from all the dangers . . . of love is Hell.[15]

If the vulnerability of love opens the door for pain, but closing the door carries a price too high to pay, the dilemma of relationship appears permanent and insoluble.

The simple statement "I'm sorry" offers the potential for a kind of humility that reconciles some of the potential for brokenness inherent in all relationships at the same time that it shows me the consequences of feeling omnipotent. When I seek to make things right, leaving my gift at the altar and asking for reconciliation with an offended person,[16] I surrender part of my need for power, laying down the weapons of self-righteousness and self-justification to apologize and ask forgiveness. The same courtesy extends to those who offend me.[17] In the process of individual or mutual apology, personal power is diminished. I put myself essentially at the mercy of the other, making her or him my judge with the right either to acquit or to convict me. In a sense, the wounded party becomes God's partner in the exchange, representing what we deserve. Forgiveness, as a form of grace, gives me what I need instead. In the process, I humble myself, relinquishing my illusory hold on personal power to receive something much better in exchange: the fruit of the Spirit.

"I Need You"

Admitting weakness runs the risk of judgment and even ridicule from others. During a long season when Janet and I were not pastoring a church and were working in warehouses and offices, I came to understand in very concrete terms the penalties for living off the radar. With the exception of a few friends, our contacts with the ministerial world simply dried up almost overnight. Looking for a new pastorate devolved into an exercise in explaining to search committees why our employment status (delivering interoffice mail for Digital, working in the post office of a Catholic college) was *not* evidence of unfitness to serve. After all, if we deserved a role in vocational ministry, what were we doing working in a warehouse? One night, in the midst of this trial, having sent resumes all over America leading to twenty-seven consecutive turndowns, my friend Dave called and told us of an opening in a church in Florida. Three weeks later, my name appeared on their stationary as the senior pastor. I needed Dave. He possessed knowledge and perspective that eluded us in our tiny, one-bedroom apartment next to the interstate. His phone call broke our isolation and offered the opportunity to express the reality of our helplessness, in return for which we received life-giving encouragement in a season during which we were mostly treated like dead people. Just having someone care and believe we might still have something to offer helped to bring us back to life.

Reflecting on this experience, I conclude that virtually every major error in judgment on issues of guidance in my life stems from attempting to go it alone, insisting on acting as the one others depend on rather than the one who needs to depend on others. My navigational errors generally took the form of overreacting to negatives in a situation and deciding on impulse to bail out. Or turning my back on an opportunity that did not seem to offer a perfectly safe path into the future (in other words, it scared me). Both types of error share the feature of personal isolation. I avoided the difficult and sometimes embarrassing process of going to "many advisors" for help and so temporarily sheltered my pride and my fear, but I deprived myself of the very assets needed to make a good choice.[18]

I paid the price for my independence for years, until the pain grew sufficiently to force me to say, "I need you." This simple phrase automatically extends my assets to include all those to whom I say it. The team environment of the doctoral program I direct for my denomination's seminary is a case study in this sort of mutual dependence. Cheryl, Lori, Steven, and Tracy make me look better than I am by bringing things to the table that I simply cannot supply. All teams are a work in progress, but ours depends on me (as the team leader) taking a deep breath and saying "I need you" to these extraordinary people. Every time I find a way to communicate this kind of respect for my teammates, we get better at what we do. God uses their gifts and their wisdom to help me, and to humble me enough to admit that none of us is complete without the rest of us, that real power comes from collaborating in a community in which no one except Christ holds the starring role. Saying "I need you" crucifies my impersonation of omnipresence (as well as omniscience and omnipotence), opening the way for a kind of humility that brings isolated individuals together into healthy communities.

Imperfect Humility and How I Attained It

The nature of human beings involves the desire to be more than we are, a desire easily corrupted into a dangerous extension of our knowledge, power, and presence. If these extensions go far enough, you may delude yourself into thinking that "you will be like God knowing good and evil."[19] Pride, then, inflates autobiography, my story, as if it told the tale of the whole world, as if the teller's perspective rises to the status of metanarrative—the big story that explains all the little ones, the way all the applications in your computer depend on an operating system. Humility represents the opposite, realizing the futility of one's own knowledge, power, and presence; I decrease my story, as John did, so that it fits within the story of Christ. With John, I stand by rejoicing as friends of the bridegroom hearing his voice at last.

Living a humble life involves choice but requires much more, beginning with a strong sense of who and what I am *not*, and then taking the form of a vocabulary that constantly sensitizes me to my limits and, in so doing, invites the Holy Spirit to change my heart.

My sense of centrality decreases, and the influence of Jesus within me increases. The preacher on the other end of my FM car radio preset button rejoices not in the bridegroom's voice but in his own. A life representing an attitude of "I know!" "You're wrong!" and "You need me!" serves as what my friend Glen calls a "blocker," standing in the way of the spiritually hungry rather than motivating them to investigate Jesus further. This kind of prideful voice is so big that the Jesus he presents shrinks into a form too small and too mean to generate curiosity, let alone hunger. The person searching for God needs a Jesus large enough to transcend all the individual stories represented by followers who know, like John, that they only prepare the way.

Part Two

Organizational Disciplines

Chapter Seven

Assessment

The Discipline of Missional Efficiency

The Diedrich Coffee House was a thing of beauty—outdoor patio, birds flitting, and West Coast cool. I arrived there late in the afternoon armed with a borrowed Super-8 video camera to interview Ted, whose shaved head and earrings made him a virtual poster boy for the emerging church leaders among whom I was embedded at the time. Ted completed the look with his "church clothes": baggy cargo shorts and a T-shirt. The striking thing about him, however, was not his sense of style but his articulate and forthcoming answers to my questions about his church and the urban/beach/college culture it served.

With one exception. "How much of your congregation is here because they have come to faith, rather than by some kind of transfer from another church?" I asked. After blanching for a second, Ted quickly recovered his cool and gave me an honest answer: he didn't really know, but he suggested I attend the next worship service at the church and make my own judgment. An hour later, I walked into a rented nursing home auditorium packed with twentysomethings and spent two hours taping and interviewing anyone willing to talk to me. But I could make no judgment about where they came from; they were all dressed like Ted.

I remember Ted so distinctly because he represents many of the leaders I interviewed during site visits. On only a couple of occasions did a pastor of any sort of church answer my question with a degree of confidence. Ted and the others surprised me not with their responses but because they were apparently overlooking this issue until my question came along, a kind of blindness I experienced for myself as a pastor. This chapter argues that missional outcomes cannot be realized without the off-road practice of treating assessment of our ministry as a spiritual discipline, the one that asks, "Are we participating in expanding the Kingdom of God, or just rearranging it? Are we doing God's will well?"

What Gets Done Gets Measured

Harvard's Robert Behn observes that " 'what gets measured gets done' is perhaps the most famous aphorism of performance measurement."[1] This slogan becomes bottom-line reality in accountability techniques ranging from 360-degree reviews to old-fashioned monthly sales figures. But performance measurement does more than produce numbers for stockholder reports. The metrics employed by an organization have a way of focusing its attention and resources on the goals those measurements are tied to, regardless of whether the goals have merit or not. So when we measure, we need to take extra care that we are evaluating things that need and deserve it, not just the things that are easiest to count.

The Church often adopts the language of business without the substance. For example, ministries understand themselves as pursuing a high calling in the abstract, but in practical terms they experience *assessment drift*, the failure to capitalize on the power of concentrated effort because no common benchmark calls the group forward into action. Church growth and evangelism expert George G. Hunter III laments the result: "The crisis of our time is that at least eight out of ten churches have not yet decided whether they intend to compete for the minds and hearts of human beings."[2] Having little notion of what they *should* be doing, there is no basis on which to conclude that it is or is not happening. In fact, most churches have little idea where they stand in regard to critical measurements of effectiveness, whether or not they know what those measurements are.

Assessment drift also arises out of the tendency to interpret the "mystery" of a revealed faith as applying to its practices and outcomes. Two schools of thought prevail here. One retreats into purely qualitative standards such as obedience and faithfulness as the only plausible metrics for subjective, spiritual issues. An alternative approach questions the spiritual legitimacy of evaluation itself. The sacredness of the core Christian message naturally extends, in the minds of some, to the means by which it is expressed, making assessment a spiritual misdemeanor at best and an act of presumption at worst. Who are *we* to evaluate what God wants to do through us?

Neither the practical nor the spiritual objections to assessment, however, mean that no evaluation takes place. Most ministries simply invert the iron law of performance evaluation; for them, what gets done gets measured. In other words, like all organizations, ministries tend to back their evaluative standards out of their current activities, generally using metrics that describe the status quo such as attendance, budgets, and the like. This approach contributes to *assessment shift* (working hard at the wrong kinds of measurement), which constitutes the mainstream of ministry performance measurement today.

Standards such as attendance and finance demand attention for obvious reasons. However, the suggestion that these yardsticks, even in combination, sufficiently describe a ministry's faithfulness to its core mission lacks a foundation in Scripture and experience. In fact, all these metrics run the risk of *objectification*, assigning a quantitative value to something as qualitative as the spiritual life of a ministry. Writing in the context of individual performance review for highly creative people, for example, leadership experts Vijay Govindarajan and Chris Trimble ask the critical question: "In the face of such complexity, do you want to motivate *only* what is measurable?"[3] Christian leaders need to ask the same question, but they seldom do.

Statistical measurement addresses the important issue of what we are doing, but it neglects the more important question of why we are doing it. If the *why* question lacks priority, the *what* question ultimately tells us very little, and the potential of performance management to guide the ministry dissipates.

Quantitative measures function indistinctly from those used by a company manufacturing energy drinks or microchips. In other words, they are cultural benchmarks derived more from context than from a sense of how the ministry meaningfully reflects God's Kingdom. So, how do we know what we are measuring? Does attendance growth indicate that we are having a "revival," or that a nearby congregation's troubles fuel growth at our church?[4] Does a budget increase speak to the grace of sacrificial giving, or to the arrival of a major donor who expects special treatment?

Carl, a pastor friend, told me recently of a group of newcomers to his thriving church who invited him to a lunch meeting. The group sought to buy more than a midday meal, expressing their intention to join the congregation and start tithing immediately from their substantial incomes—provided the pastor made certain "changes" in the church. Carl refused, and the potential members (with their potential donations) moved on, presumably looking for a leader with less integrity to accommodate their tastes. Carl's acceptance of the offer would have held the potential to make his ministry more "effective" by several cultural benchmarks, perhaps earning him conference speaking engagements. But would any of this represent the heart of God for His community?

Ironically, ministry leaders who lean almost exclusively on quantitative measurement sometimes admonish believers weekly, in one form or another, to live out things like the "greatest commandment" of loving God and others.[5] Management professor and corporate vice president Steven Kerr refers to this as "the folly of rewarding A while hoping for B."[6] In other words, we encourage others to live spiritually while measuring only the practical. The lesson is not lost on those being led. Researcher George Barna declares: "The axiom 'you get what you measure' is certainly true for the Christian body in the U.S. Until we start to think about, pursue, and measure genuine spiritual transformation in individual lives, we will continue to get what we've been getting, as unsatisfying as that is, for years to come."[7] In light of these comments, maybe you can see why I was frustrated when my congregation invited Christian friends to an "outreach" event like an Easter production. Attendance at the service was the only thing we counted, other than professions of faith, which were unlikely given the preference for Christian visitors that my measurement scheme encouraged.

WWJM (What Would Jesus Measure)?

Jesus seems so often to specialize in the invisible, the heart issues that shape every form of attitude and behavior. Although modern leadership writers[8] have described Him in terms of a CEO, an entrepreneur, and a life coach, it's hard to imagine a CEO addressing a stockholder or board of directors meeting with these words: "Do not store up for yourselves treasures on earth, where moth and rust destroy, and where thieves break in and steal. But store up for yourselves treasures in heaven, where moth and rust do not destroy, and where thieves do not break in and steal."[9]

Clearly, Jesus is using metrics that diverge sharply from those backed out of culture. How might He instruct us to assess our ministries so as to use the world's metrics appropriately, but not remain beholden to them?

Not Everything That Needs Doing Needs Measuring

The Pharisees of Jesus' time were experts at measured religion. Hundreds of rules provided almost infinite opportunities to evaluate the righteousness of others publicly. They loved scorekeeping because it fed their self-righteousness and enhanced their power. I can know if you went to church last Sunday (and can use absence to make you feel guilty), but I'm a lot less likely to know if you resent a more-talented coworker, or if you lack self-control in your thought life. Rule-based religionists reduce the grace of God to a ticket admitting us to a life of observing their regulations. That's why we call them *legalists*.

Jesus drove them crazy. When He encountered both the woman at the well[10] and the woman caught in adultery,[11] He did not hesitate to confront the issues in their lives, although the Pharisees would have been horrified that He even spoke to the former and actually sought Him out to impose a death sentence on the latter. He told the truth about both (but kept no scorecard), dispensing grace rather than judgment. He gave them what they *needed* instead of what they *deserved*.

So the first thing Jesus might do is *not* measure certain things. For example, He would not regard worship attendance as love for God, a small donation as lack of generosity, or religious-sounding phrases as true worship. "And when you pray," He taught, "do not be like the hypocrites, for they love to pray standing in the synagogues and on the street corners to be seen by men. I tell you the truth, they have received their reward in full."[12] This sort of measurement blindness keeps spiritual issues where they belong—in the heart—and helps to avoid secular or religious reductionism, which would make assessment little more than a matter of the bottom line or scorekeeping legalism.

What Is the Top Line?

Some Christian leaders shy away from assessment of any sort. I suspect this reluctance springs from two roots: their own insecurities and doubts about the effectiveness (or spirituality) of the methods themselves. Neither issue hindered Jesus. His followers reported back to Him after their ministry ventures in teams of two. Similarly, Paul and Barnabas planned on returning to the churches founded in their earlier missionary travels to "see how they are doing." Paul had similar intentions for the church at Rome.[13] Of course, the statistics reported in the gospels and the book of Acts[14] indicate that someone paid attention (though claiming that they represent a first-century version of a modern, business-style ledger changes the meaning of these texts into something unrecognizable).

The real source of assessment for Christian leaders therefore becomes not the world's bottom line but the Kingdom's top line, the fact that a moment of ultimate accountability with Jesus awaits all of us: "For we will all stand before God's judgment seat."[15] Written in the context of issues of conscience, Paul's argument is that our presumption to judge one another (legalism) has been trumped by Christ's absolute right to judge us all.[16] Paul's words underline the importance of what we are not measuring (others' spirituality) and what we are measuring (our own responsibility).

Bono of U2 offers a pointed example of what it means to call the Church to accountability in light of this day:

> I mean, what is going on with the churches? It is incredible. I tell these evangelicals in the United States there are 2,300 verses of scripture about the poor. It's the central message outside of personal redemption, the idea of dealing with the poor. And I'm asking them, where are they? Where are they on this? On a recent poll of evangelical churches, only six per cent said they wanted to do something about AIDS. It is unbelievable, the leprosy of our time if you like. But it's starting to turn; the Church is starting to wake up.[17]

Let's hope so. Jesus spoke to this issue in Matthew 25, describing a judgment of the nations at which He will "separate the people one from another as a shepherd separates the sheep from the goats."[18] The basis of this division has nothing to do with observance of religious rules or corporate benchmarks, but with whether or not we help the helpless. As He identified with our pain and alienation on the cross, He expects us to identify with the marginalized in our community. Jesus Himself is both the beginning and the end of accountability for the Church.

Missional Efficiency

A surprising number of the pastors I meet in the course of a year confess privately that they long to do something more "spiritual." This remark sounds odd or even offensive. By definition, pastoral ministry represents a spiritual calling of the first order, one of the leadership gifts that Jesus left the Church. But at least some Christian leaders I encounter labor with an unfulfilled longing to do ministry in a way that feels more like co-laboring with Christ than being employed by Christians. Ironically, I think many Christians (especially lay leaders) feel exactly the same way, regretting what pastor Bill Hull calls "a leadership model that insists pastors be managers of church growth rather than shepherds helping people go deeper into the life Christ has for us."[19] If we opened a dialogue on this issue using assessment as the platform, who knows what might become possible?

This discussion could evolve from the notion that accountability begins not with measurement in any form but with *identification*. Jesus Himself represents the standard for the Church of which He is also "the head"[20] and the "chief cornerstone."[21] The top line is the extent to which we are individually or corporately conformed to His image.[22] Are we fully committed to loving God and others with everything that we are? If you are like me, the answer varies with the day.

This form of spiritual assessment is complex, involving appropriate forms of statistical measurement but including much more than that. Many leaders in the business community prefer a method called the "balanced scorecard" in situations like this. Conventional pencil-and-paper measures, they argue, permit an important but retrospective analysis, offering little insight into where things need to go from here. Moreover, reducing performance measurement to a function of bookkeeping tends to undervalue soft operational assets such as creativity, emotional intelligence, and morale, which have huge long-term implications.[23]

The compound-measurement model affords Christian ministries a significant opportunity to evaluate themselves rigorously but spiritually, *and* to obey God in shaping their future, since, as Regent University business professor George Babbes points out, "for ministries . . . that leading [of the Holy Spirit] is always front and center on the scorecard."[24] Pastor and educator Greg Ogden, for example, suggests application of this principle to forming disciples.[25] On the congregational level, author and leadership expert Reggie McNeal argues: "Adopting a missionary approach will require changing the scorecard. Church scorecards currently reflect member values: how many show up, pay up, and participate in club member activities. These are the numbers used to compare one church with another—the numbers that denominations ask for in their reports. These numbers establish the pecking order among clergy. The bigger the better and the more respected by club members of other churches."[26]

There is little question that this characterization of the secular, status-quo–oriented metric is true much too often. So the notion of applying some form of balanced scorecard to ministry needs serious attention. Until new metrics are in place, I see little hope that any other tweaks to a ministry's culture will prove enduring.

But what would a scorecard look like? I want to suggest one example as a starting point for congregational ministry. Any scorecard is context-bound and prone to its own shortcomings. But we seek to discern an approximation of the ministry of Jesus, not an utterly precise rendition of our best ideas. This identification with Jesus always makes the ministry more missional, aiming it for the margins with Jesus at the center, rather than us at the center and Jesus at the margins. Our metrics need not be perfect to tell the difference between these two states. Moreover, leaders working together to discern the operations of the Spirit in their midst are going to find a way, even if the scorecard must be totally replaced in the process. The point is not the scorecard, but the discipline of spiritual assessment that it promotes.

I think of such a scorecard as representing "missional efficiency." The core issue being assessed concerns how closely we are identifying with Christ, co-laboring with Him, being sent by Him just as He has been sent by the Father. Hopefully, a scorecard something like this example challenges leaders to think, pray, and act in a way more noticeably identified with Jesus. The items suggest general categories of concern in the parish context. I assume here that the organization already monitors the statistical basics such as finance:

1. What proportion of our largest group meeting (and our leadership) is present because of a significant faith experience, rather than by transfer?

2. What proportion of our leadership did we develop here by spiritual formation and leadership training?

3. What have we learned about doing ministry in our context in the last month? What have we done about it?

4. How many spiritual conversations have we had this month with unchurched (marginalized) people?

5. What would our church look like if we had the same income but the majority of it came from those under thirty (or the poor, or the unchurched)?

6. What would our ministry look like if the pre-Christian community had a representative with veto power on our board of directors?

7. If we worked for a missions agency, would we still have jobs?

8. What are the best stories we can tell about the things God has done among us since our last meeting?

9. What would we say to a poor person who asked us what we have done to help the marginalized since our last meeting?

10. Who is growing spiritually among us, and how do we know this?

The nonnegotiable feature of performance measurement is not the exact questions used but the fact that questions are even asked. These ten suggest some possible beginning points to design your own.

Truth Telling

The most important commitment of performance measurement involves telling the truth. Knowing what not to measure and understanding the delicate balance of quantitative and qualitative metrics are vital, as is rigorous use of a specific set of evaluative criteria. The goal of these off-road practices is to bring the ministry into identification with the mission of Christ. However, Jesus' presence among us changes everything, often revealing some uncomfortable realities. The test comes not in creating a scorecard (anyone can) but in having the courage to say the truth out loud once we've got one. Bill Hull relates an example from his own pastoral ministry, referring to a Sunday on which eighty-three members joined his church. Most of us would rejoice at the prospect, but Hull could not because he realized that his impressive organizational work was not producing transformed lives. So on that Sunday, he asked the congregation, " 'Why should we bring eighty-three new people into something that isn't working?' It was the first time in thirty years of ministry I had admitted something I was leading wasn't working. It appeared to be working, but it just wasn't."[27]

The transformation of Hull's church began with this statement on a Sunday morning and the personal struggle that led to it. As in most ministries, change usually begins in painful truth. If I lack the nerve to admit that my best efforts fall far short, the idea of top-line performance measurement based on identification with Christ and His mission will remain only theory. Here we part company with cultural metrics, be they secular or religious. Neither asks me to humble myself. Neither focuses me on the right things. Neither holds out a hope of growing a ministry that someone from the outside might recognize as representing Jesus.

Chapter Eight

Harmony

The Discipline of Blending Differences

Larry wept openly. The pressure of holding together the churches in his region spilled out into our classroom, along with his deep concern that even the best efforts of the regional leadership lacked whatever it takes to bring unity. As the chief administrator of one geographic area for his denomination, Larry (whom we met in Chapter Six) spent many hours either managing conflict within a congregation or defusing conflict with some pastor who found the ministry of other pastors intolerable. The former sort of power struggle goes with the territory. But the latter, fratricidal confrontation, seemed particularly enervating for a man who cared so deeply about spiritual leaders.

As we spent a week together in a class of about fifteen leaders, Larry referred to one account after another of potential fratricide, one family member attempting to harm another. Two typical scenarios emerged from our dialogue. One involved a "hard-line" pastor confronting Larry about the conduct of a nontraditional leader or congregation with this sort of question: "How long are you going to let this sort of thing go on?" Larry was supposed to respond by coming down hard on those who seemed to threaten the denomination's identity by watering down its distinctives or twisting its practices into something alien. The other scenario took the form of more progressive leaders simply withdrawing from his region's activities despite their personal respect for Larry's team and his countless hours spent reassuring them of his support. These clashes represented much more than a division between old and young. As

Larry pointed out, they resulted more from ideology than from demographics. The active confrontations Larry managed drained his energy, but I sensed that the passive withdrawals broke his heart. They meant that a bright leader was opting out of the organization to which Larry had devoted his long professional life.

The one consistent element of these conflicts, however, involved Larry finding himself in the middle, using his considerable diplomatic skills to absorb the arrows fired by the hard-liners while reaching out to what might be called the soft-liners. The latter group never saw the punishment he took on their behalf, sometimes assuming the organization offered them no seats at the table without asking. Meanwhile their hard-line brothers and sisters assumed that Larry was soft on critical issues of doctrine and identity. Both sides were breathtakingly wrong.

This chapter contends that working toward the kind of harmony Larry seeks is more likely if we think of the task as an off-road spiritual discipline. Getting along is a relationship that springs from a state of mind, not an event that draws its life from joint meetings or ceremonies, as useful as those elements can be. In Christ, we have received both the "ministry of reconciliation" and the "message of reconciliation."[1] Whether (or how) we apply them to the crisis of fratricidal conflict is up to us.

Two Impulses, One Church

For those who prefer dealing in stereotypes, let's say that fratricide in the Church springs from clashes between moderns and postmoderns, the young and the old, or baby boomers and gen Xers. Though these conflicts occur too often, they represent symptoms of an underlying divergence (one of many) present in the Church since its first hours. The conflict stems from the challenge of forming one Church out of two competing impulses, one demanding *preservation* and one calling for *innovation*. At least some of Church history, and much of our current crisis, results from the tension between the two poles.

Claiming roots in the witness of the Scriptures, the preservation impulse contends for "the faith that was once for all entrusted to the saints."[2] From this perspective, the primary issue for the Church concerns theological and doctrinal purity, the raw material from which each generation forges a new link in the unbroken chain of Christian experience as its legacy for the next. Failure to fulfill this sacred obligation is, from the preservationist viewpoint, a serious betrayal of trust. The ongoing ministry of the body of Christ depends for its effectiveness on maintaining spotless orthodoxy, meaning that any form of ineffectiveness in its culture likely results from some corruption of the true faith, correction of which creates a "revival." After all, didn't Paul tell the Galatians that "if anybody is preaching to you a gospel other than what you accepted, let him be eternally condemned!"?[3] The risk of diluting the gospel, then, can spark a defensive attitude when change looms, even if the issues involved appear relatively minor. Such forms of ministry as worship services and church government serve as the guardians of truth. During our discussions, Larry pointed out that this ideology makes sense if we consider that what we *do* becomes what we *are* over many years. Those serving God in a certain way for most of a lifetime naturally assume that their way represents a sacred path that deserves conservation. Changing it means giving up on not just favored methods but a whole way of life.

With biblical passages in tow, the preservationist argues passionately to minimize change in the Church's current approach to ministry (regardless of what that might be) and often regards tinkering with it as deeply threatening. The inclusion of the Gentiles from the Roman provinces into the Christian faith initially centered in Jerusalem, for example, brought this clash into high relief in the early Church.[4] Even the decision to admit them left unresolved the issue of whether "the gentiles must be circumcised and required to obey the Law of Moses."[5] Conservatives contended that the path into Christianity for Gentiles went through Judaism— that is, Gentile converts should be required to undergo the covenant sign spelled out in the Law cherished by the Jews. For those close to the preservation impulse, maintaining these scriptural customs represented the best way to protect the witness of Christ for the long haul; the Law guards the gospel.

The main challenge for preservationists, however, arises when something more than the core issues of orthodoxy is in view. Where do the hard truths that define Christianity end and the soft truths of conscience begin?[6] Ironically, preservationists have frequently disagreed among themselves on the list of hard truths constituting orthodoxy. Calvinists and Arminians both regard themselves as orthodox, but they hold differing views of grace and salvation. I have met representatives of both camps who evangelize more for their perspective than they do for the gospel. This divergence can motivate all sides to hold on even tighter to their points of view. In the worst-case scenario, a religious war starts between two schools of orthodoxy. In happier times, the result is only an irony: creation of a sort of pluralism among preservationists—a state they generally despise but in which they are trapped by the heterogeneous nature of those practicing Christian orthodoxy.

A second irony involves the elasticity with which something as precious (and as static) as absoluteness attaches itself to issues beyond doctrine, such as worship style, church structure, wardrobe, color of paint in a bathroom, and so on. Of course, for preservationists no such ironies occur since their views putatively mirror the plain teaching of Scripture, meaning that anyone reading the Bible "correctly" and using a commonsense form of interpretation ought to come to the same conclusion.

The preservationist practice of what I call "orthodoxy creep" tends to doctrinalize everything it touches, freighting small issues with theological significance. In his *Lectures on Revival*, for instance, Charles Finney notes the strong resistance to using the bass fiddle in nineteenth-century church services, lest one of Satan's instruments find its way into God's house.[7] From this perspective, many proposed adjustments to the Church's thinking or practice form yet another slippery slope leading downward to heresy, failure, or both, making the defense of orthodoxy (and orthopraxy) a sacred mission, sometimes even a crusade.

The innovative impulse represents a completely different orientation toward faith, asking not just "Are we orthodox in doctrine?" but "Are we effective in culture?" Innovationists tend to see the gospel as a narrative with unlimited cross-cultural potential, rather than a list of key ideas distilled from that story by a handful of expensive experts. They point out that the same apostle who warned against anyone who "preaches a Jesus other than the Jesus we preached"[8] also wrote that He became "all things to all men."[9] For the innovationist, this well-known passage indicates that the Christian gospel remains silent until expressed in indigenous forms that may often be nothing like the form of the message in the communicator's culture of origin (COO, as you will recall from Chapter One).

The debate at Jerusalem over defining the requirements to place on Gentile converts involved preservationists and innovationists. Paul and Barnabas, who were innovators, engaged in "sharp dispute and debate" over the issue at Antioch, leading to the final showdown in Jerusalem. During this climactic meeting, Peter, the Jew who preached to Cornelius's Gentile household, pointed out that God's unconditional acceptance of the Gentiles expressed itself in the form of cleansing from sin and the infilling of the Holy Spirit, both by faith in Christ.[10] The debate raged over the question of how much of the Church's brief heritage (Jewish in this case) needed to be treated like hard truth in order to protect an orthodoxy that was still oral in nature. Those in favor of admitting the Gentiles on an as-is basis responded that the results of preaching the gospel in their culture itself validated their inclusion with minimal, commonsense conditions (such as avoiding sexual immorality and idolatrous rituals) befitting the issues of the day.

Paradoxically, if considering the proposition that "methods change but the message does not," both sides, then and today, almost certainly would agree. But each hears this time-worn slogan in its own way because they start with contrasting assumptions about what these words mean. A methodological change for one group of preservationists I met took the form of deciding whether to serve coffee in adult Sunday school classes—an issue that touched off a brutal conflict at a church picnic. Meanwhile, the innovationist experimenting with methods considers canceling the midweek prayer meeting to try a hip-hop dance club worship service instead (many of which already exist, by the way). For those close to the preservation impulse, worshipping to a hip-hop beat *is* changing the message because the experience itself says, "Christians can be like *this*" (that is, like the world). Innovationists disagree, arguing that the look and feel of a worship style deserves a doctrine-neutral status; otherwise the Church loses all hope of expressing the gospel in culture-current forms. The danger for innovationists comes from heterodoxy creep, in which pursuit of cultural adaptation softens the core of the faith until it becomes indistinguishable in content from the surrounding context. At that point, Christ crucified ceases to be appropriately offensive, making Jesus a speed bump instead of a stumbling block who shatters all our religious expectations and offers His own life as the bridge to God.[11]

Of course, this simple dichotomy of preservation versus innovation greatly oversimplifies a complicated situation. In the real world, this opposition actually functions as more of a continuum, with an almost infinite variety of intermediate positions stretched out between the two poles. Moreover, proximity to either pole depends on the issue under consideration and the season of one's life. Peter, for example, argued strenuously for unconditional admission of the Gentiles into the Church at the Jerusalem Council (since they already participated in the Church's faith) but turned his back on the same group at Antioch, siding with the preservationists and heading toward confrontation with Paul.[12]

A final irony of Church life takes the form of the inevitable aging of even the most progressive among us, raising the possibility of one day sitting among the preservationists! I scoffed, for example, when Chad, a young leader in my fellowship, asked me recently about house churches. I know and respect many people in the movement, but my unfiltered reaction projected skepticism: "We were in house churches the first time they were tried—thirty years ago. It's hard to see hippy house church as the path forward!" My point was that we *no longer* worshipped in house churches (no longer being hippies), now preferring a more conventional, more Boomer format of music, announcements, offering, preaching, and prayer. Did I just say that? Did I just criticize a part of the body of Christ because their notion of the Church takes a different form from mine? Have I petrified into a preservationist on some issues while pleading for innovation on others as it suits me? Perhaps. No one description adequately captures a living entity like the Church, but the tension between preserving and innovating simply offers up too many examples, personal and institutional, for us to ignore. We can use this dichotomy to understand the American Church as featuring a range of three basic brands.

Three Brands, One Church

Reconciliation begins with understanding. If each segment of the Church grasps the assumptions and culture of the others, getting along seems less impossible. Studying the American Church in the twenty-first century leads me to think of at least its Anglo rendition as organized around three major philosophies, three brands within one Church: traditional, contemporary, and experimental. If we regard our current cultural perfect storm as composed of premodern, modern, and postmodern perspectives (along with many other elements) all swirling and combining in the same social space, each church philosophy can be understood as drawing on its own combination of these perspectives, thus assuming a unique look complete with advantages and disadvantages. As we would expect, examples of success and failure, however defined, abound within each brand.

Gunsmoke Nation: Traditional Church

The traditional church takes its position closest to the preservation impulse. Although in some minds the word *traditional* reduces to a label for hymns, choirs, and loud preaching, the brand actually derives its power from the idea that we inherit the best forms of ministry from the past. The congregation knows we "had church" the right way because those forms and experiences approximate the experience of twenty or fifty years ago, or wherever the group locates its favorite nostalgia point. This historical myth may revolve around a founding pastor, a legendary revival, or the practices of the church during the construction of what once represented their new building. The gravitational pull of the nostalgia point may grip the whole culture of the congregation, or only a sacred cow or two. No matter the starting place, every ministry tends to freeze its nostalgia point (or points) at some moment depicting their best and brightest memory of themselves and then evaluate future practices against this benchmark.

In this context, the leader holds the position of a prophet or commander whose credibility flows from two sources: (1) the role of *messenger* bringing the word of God down from the mountain to the people waiting below; and (2) the function of *station keeping,* holding the group as close to the nostalgia point as possible. So even though representatives of the brand look different according to the context, they share a common allegiance to heritage and cast themselves as conservators of that heritage for the good of future generations. To threaten ministry elements left to us as a sacred legacy by our predecessors often feels to traditionals like a deadly threat to a core aspect of their mission, which is to perpetuate the church as they understand it.

Deep spirituality ranks among the many positive traits of the traditional brand, along with the sacrifice and dedication that created the ministry infrastructure on which much of the church still relies. Drawing on the values of the builder generation (the folks who won World War II), this form of ministry tends to emphasize individual spiritual disciplines, as well as offer opportunities for corporate intercession and service. However, their preservationist bent means they struggle with openness to the outside culture. Like the conservatives at the Jerusalem Council, the traditionals' great strength of cherishing historic forms of the faith translates poorly at times into welcoming those to whom those forms mean little. The traditional brand, then, can be thought of as the Jerusalem church, the church of the founders, evolving in a largely monocultural rural context and bent on preserving the truth.

In *The Postmodern World*, theologian Millard Erickson suggests that the values of this traditional brand become clearer if we associate it with a television program that represents the builder generation culture of origin.[13] Erickson offers *Gunsmoke*, a popular western of the 1960s and early 1970s, as his cultural exemplar. In that TV series, Marshall Matt Dillon wore a white hat in his weekly quest to rid Dodge City of bad men in black hats. The showdown in the street that culminated many episodes stands as a paradigm for the traditional brand, which holds black-and-white values and understands power as the way to ensure that right triumphs over wrong. Thus the Jerusalem church taps into an "I believe therefore I see" perspective on faith, a core concept of the premodern worldview and the bedrock of its affinity for preservation.

Frasier Nation: The Contemporary Church

In between the preservation and innovation impulses, practitioners of the contemporary church brand refuse to look exclusively to the past for ministry forms, preferring to emulate their more successful peers. This brand arrives along with post–World War II suburbanization and the baby boomers who grew up in those suburbs and now constitute 60 percent of America's senior pastors. We boomers know one thing for sure: we do not want to be like our parents. We try to sanitize this sentiment by calling it the "generation gap," but our attitude toward preservation looks more like a gash than a gap. For us, the leader serves as a CEO or coach whose credibility stems from her or his ability to deliver results. So, if our parents responded to low Sunday night worship attendance by holding a prayer meeting on Saturday night, we reacted by canceling the event, viewing it as wasting scarce resources rather than a sacred responsibility. When in search of new ministry ideas, we attend conferences put on by admired members of our cohort, buy their products, and use them to connect the gospel message to our frenetic, suburbanized context. However, in the process the contemporaries tend to stay conservative theologically, being close enough to the preservation impulse to remain quite traditional in their doctrinal views.

The pragmatism of the contemporaries offers a major advantage to the Church. This brand, for example, applied the word *model* to ministry for the first time and brings study of the leadership arts to bear on the Church, with a consistent focus on growing ministries and designing processes to disciple people. The philosophy here resonates with modernity in that it revolves around our ability to understand our context by research, manipulate it by intentionality, and generate predictable results by design. So discipleship looks for a contemporary, not like the desert fathers practicing silent meditation in a mountain cave but like cohorts of people being moved along the path of a baseball diamond, 101, 201, 301. . . . Process is king.

The contemporary brand offers the ability to escape traditional ministry approaches that consume resources without producing fruitfulness, which means that the paper bulletin becomes a Web page, Sunday school is replaced by small groups, and Sunday night becomes "family time." But even though these assumptions make wonderful servants, they make terrible masters. The desire to control outcomes resembles the world around us so much that it makes it difficult to see anything *uniquely* Christian in our efforts. Moreover, the depth of spiritual experiences packaged into highly produced and painstakingly managed events needs evaluation. If God decided to do something off the script (as with Jesus' confrontation with the demonized man in the synagogue at Capernaum[14]), would we let him do so during one of our scripted services? The contemporary brand represents the church at Antioch, the first major city where Jewish Christians engaged Gentiles in quantity, a bicultural atmosphere in which new believers came from a completely different starting point, outside the envelope of Jewish experience. In this environment, contemporaries work out ministry in fully modern terms that traditionals only partly embrace. The latter believe we need to wait on God; the former think God is waiting on us.

Erickson suggests that this type of culture finds televised expression in *Frasier*, a sitcom about two boomer psychiatrists, Niles and Frasier Crane, who, with their father Martin, explore life and loneliness. Each episode involves the two sons pressing the limits of both ethics and morality (for example, lying to each other) and then sorting out how to repair the damage, all the while feeling guilty. These two professionals possess world-class training but seem unable to save themselves from themselves. Like the boomers they represent, their tools for controlling the world never seem quite adequate to order their own lives. From another perspective, Niles and Frasier have just enough religion to make them miserable.

The contemporary brand, with its emphasis on size (represented in the megachurch it popularized), felt-need teaching ("Communicating with Your Teenager"), and culture-current worship ("If pop music sounds like U2, our worship will sound like U2"), speaks the language of the suffering modern seeker, of Frasier, who just wants his life to work but has no idea how. Operating from an "I see therefore I believe" perspective, contemporaries appeal to the modern seeker who weighs the evidence, both practical and philosophical, as a path to faith. The contemporary brand offers Frasier the chance to connect to God through his needs and questions, just as the traditional brand makes the same offer to Matt Dillon through its heritage and claims of biblical truth.

Seinfeld Nation: The Experimental Church

The experimental church holds the position closest to the innovative impulse.[15] Unlike the retrospective traditionals or the peer-based contemporaries, the experimental brand looks to culture itself for inspiration, making the leader a combination native guide and spiritual director. One of my first field research visits, for example, took me to an art lounge in Southern California. Late at night, I watched around seventy-five college-age young adults sit in rows of straight-backed chairs transfixed by local performance artists reciting poetry, singing folk songs, and generally expressing their art in street terms. The leaders of the ministry simply concluded that their location in an art colony demanded that they provide a vehicle for the artistic expression native to the area, leading eventually to spiritual conversation that attracted the locals to their faith community. This particular venue, as with most among the experimentals, drew its leadership from the youngest adults, often those we might call cultural creatives, who live at the evolving edge of urban life by creating and consuming it. As one Silicon Valley consultant described his region to me, "We invent the world here." Being a native of an area like this makes cultural understanding natural for experimentals, though it must be learned by representatives of the other brands. Raised in the Internet generation, for example, my friend Tim created e-church out of the raw material native to his culture. He speaks Web the way I speak English.

The beauty of experimentation finds expression in the open architecture of its method. The innovative impulse drives adaptation to culture in any form in which we find it, a skill that some cross-cultural leaders value in every era of the Church's life, whether Hudson Taylor among the Chinese or a retired businesswoman moving to the inner city to work at a free clinic. The fluidity of postmodern culture (probably the closest thing to a defining trait) makes the ability to morph along with it an indispensable skill, and one readily available to natives. So, for example, many of my friends in the experimental brand value "excellence" but treasure "authenticity." There is no being right without being real. My own contemporary brand tends to push excellence to the front, with authenticity becoming the responsibility of small-group leaders or relegated to self-deprecating humor used to introduce a sermon.

Constant morphing, however, carries the risk factor of absorption into the very culture the gospel seeks to transform. Paul, the apostle who wanted to be "all things to all men," for example, chastised the Corinthian church for permitting immorality "of a kind that does not even occur among pagans."[16] This and other flaws in the early Church resulted not from an abstraction like the postmodern worldview but from an enmeshment in culture that overwhelmed the body of Christ's immune system, so to speak, until its health deteriorated. A second risk factor for experimentals shows up in the checkbook. The youthfulness of this brand means that the desire for innovation almost always outstrips the resources available to make it possible. In other words, the experimentals tend to lack venture capital to bring their dreams of a culturally intelligible church to fruition. For this reason, I think of the experimental brand as the potential church of Spain referred to by Paul in Romans 15. After preaching the gospel throughout Asia Minor, Paul writes to the Roman church of his desire to visit with them on his way to places where no one has heard the message of Jesus, specifically Spain, a region considered the province of barbarians. No one knows if Paul made it to Spain, and no one knows the prospects of the experimental brand of church.

Erickson suggests *Seinfeld* as the television icon of the culture to which the experimental church appeals. As the "show about nothing" driven by two negative rules (no touching, no learning) this comedy speaks as an early example of a postmodern perspective, which features the defining trait of having no defining trait. One episode features Kramer, Jerry Seinfeld's neighbor, setting up the junked set of the Merv Griffin show in his apartment to host a pseudotelevision program complete with human and animal guests. This absurdist format, mixed with plot lines majoring in trivia and a scathing treatment of older people, mocks both the heritage of the traditionalist and the intentionality of the contemporary view of life, suggesting exploration as the only alternative.

The openness of the experimental brand (with its many subbrands, ranging from Ancient-Future worship to Cyberchurch) resonates with cultural natives who find traditionals too exclusive and inflexible and contemporaries too controlling and inauthentic. The truth is that everything you believe about the experimental church is true—somewhere. Briefly, I have catalogued four basic life forms among the experimentals, most of which tend to be led by people in their twenties and thirties:

- *Turbo church.* These congregations generally are led by twentysomethings but use the market-adapted techniques of contemporary church to attract young adults, resulting in sermons preached by pastors wearing shorts and T-shirts, music that sounds like Coldplay, and fun new titles ("I'm not the Senior Pastor, you understand, I'm the Spiritual Experience Facilitator").
- *Gap ministries.* Often using turbo-style methods, these groups usually take the shape of subministries within contemporary churches, representing an effort on the part of older leaders to furnish a spiritual home for otherwise disenfranchised twentysomethings. Large churches create young adult "gap" ministries for the same reason they create youth ministries. The groups differ from turbo churches in structure (congregation versus subministry) and in motivation (outreach versus filling a demographic void).
- *Alternative church.* The first question in these shops is not how to adapt to the market but how to explore our faith together. "Community" tends to be the priority as the group searches for new ways to discover and live Christianity. This process of discovery is often referred to as a "journey" or "conversation," to avoid the trappings of power seen as inherent in the turbo or gap life forms, but it all takes place within a fairly conservative notion of orthodoxy.
- *Dissident church.* These ministries disdain talk of strategy, tending to see most of the mechanics of the turbo or gap church as cosmetically disguised intruders from the contemporary brand. These groups are not just revising methods; they are protesting the corruption of the faith by what could generally be called modernity (that is, historical-critical hermeneutic, emphasis on control and power, monologue-style communication, and corporate methods).

They mean to make the rediscovery of Christianity their method, embracing the possibility of morphing the message in ways that give conservative evangelicals fits.

Obviously, even the experimental brand is beginning to develop its own subbrands, complete with both preservationist and innovationist impulses. However, the common feature of the brand is to offer Kramer a connection to God through its willingness to let everyone contribute to a greater or lesser extent to the agenda of the ministry. Pastor and writer Doug Pagitt offers an example in his congregation's practice of developing sermons using a small-group process and then doing sermons together using a large-group process he calls "progressional dialogue."[17] Traditionals and contemporaries may resist this approach as too risky, placing too much control in the hands of the untrained. Honestly, the whole idea makes me nervous too, but when I close my eyes I can see Kramer's face in the crowd.

One Lord, One Mission, One Church

Describing the American Church in the sweeping terminology of brands offers opportunity for both clarity (Where would your life or organization fall on the continuum?) and confusion (How do ethnicity and geography fit in?). So even though a branding analysis possesses serious limits, the perspective helps us step outside our experience of the Church for a moment to see it from another angle, one other than the perspective we live with every day. I routinely meet young people with traditional values, older people with an experimental take on things, and many leaders who think of themselves as experimental but build ministries in a *contemporary nouveau* genre that adopts experimental affectations to put a modern ministry on turbo. The enormous diversity lurking below the surface of this diagram almost defies description.

Many conference participants, after seeing this particular map, say, "You've just explained my children to me." But somehow this recognition of differences and their sources needs to grow into a form

Experimental (present)	Contemporary (peers)	Traditional (past)
	Modern	
Postmodern		Premodern
Spain	Antioch	Jerusalem
Seinfeld	*Frasier*	*Gunsmoke*
Native guide, Spiritual director	CEO, coach	Prophet, commander

Innovate ← ——————————————————————— → Preserve

of reconciliation that makes it easier for us to actually "accept one another, then, just as Christ accepted you, in order to bring praise to God."[18] God will do His part. The question is whether we will do ours.

Understanding where and why we are all located on some commonly agreed-on map (mine or your own) offers a small step toward mutual understanding. Which map is in use is much less important than the *process* of mapping itself, attempting to come to some shared sense of how we relate to one another. Bill Easum and Dave Travis refer to churches as "in the box," "out of the box," and "beyond the box" on the basis of commitment to innovation.[19] Robert Webber categorizes evangelicals as "traditional," "pragmatic," and "younger" according to their generation and traits.[20] Chris Saey speaks to the issue on a personal level, describing three generations of ministers in his own family.[21] Any scheme of interpretation helps us. The average leader, however, generally operates with little sense of how and why to relate to dissimilar others, making it easier to see anyone different as an intractable enemy.

Just getting together to talk things out sounds like a reasonable idea. But bringing the brands together without some interpretive framework risks putting a match to gasoline, creating a situation in which the hard-liners (each brand has them) ventilate views so angry and intolerant that the ensuing confrontation crushes any hope for harmony. Until everyone opens up to the possibility that their brand is just that—one way among many of embodying the mission of Jesus in a specific context—dialogue holds as much potential for division as for tolerance. Part of Larry's stress, in fact, stemmed from managing enough ugly, Apple-versus-Microsoft-style brand conflicts to know that a cultural Armageddon was not impossible among the churches in his region. In a listening session with around fifty young leaders from his area, a small-group process turned up the same basic concern from all of them: How are the generations going to get along?

But even warring computer manufacturers manage to sell their machines without destroying their users. They simply arrive at ways of coexisting in the form of common technical standards (e.g., nearly identical keyboard layouts on PCs and Macs) and then proceed to do business the way they see fit. These companies never seek or achieve unity in this hypercompetitive environment, but they exemplify a certain form of harmony that contributes to the overall benefit of computer users. Survival depends on never losing sight of the person working with the machine, as I am right now, writing this chapter on my laptop seated at a little round table at a Starbucks kiosk in a grocery store. If computer makers forget about my needs (and those of millions of others), they face a grim future.

Harmony, then, blends differences for the sake of the end user. Whether musical notes overlap into a beautiful sound or high-definition television manufacturers negotiate a mutual broadcast standard, harmonious relationships possess the common feature of serving someone else. Many efforts to bring about a more unified congregation or region or denomination flounder because the painful effort seems unjustified if the only benefit amounts to reduced conflict. Jesus cast an entirely different light on the purpose of unifying his followers: "May they be brought to complete unity," he prayed, "to let the world know that you sent me and have loved them even as you have loved me."[22] Jesus asks the Father to bring us together so that those in need of good news might believe it can be found among Christians. In one sense, then, the world around us stands as the end user of our relationship with each other. That's why unity is a core element of our mission.

The initiatives launched over the centuries to overcome the problem of disunity could fill an encyclopedia. Bringing together the various brands of the Church even in a modest way in a season of tumultuous cultural change requires more than another formula or another committee. A formula tends toward such generality as to defy even the best efforts to apply it. A committee usually represents the effort of an ecumenical elite seldom reaching the grassroots intact.

Ask any church member to name an attempt to unify Christians. Almost no one can. In our final conversation at the end of five days spent working through these issues, Larry expressed this frustration: "I still don't hear what we're supposed to *do* about this." I had to agree. I didn't have the how-to part figured out, but I concurred with Larry when he said, "Diplomacy doesn't happen by accident. It happens by design." Then he added, "As a baby boomer, I want to have all of this figured out, planned out so we can control it. Maybe that's not how it works."

I had to agree again. My most powerful memory of harmony involves my Protestant pastor (also my father) openly disdaining Catholics and Catholicism. His position hardened over the years into a kind of scorn that produced boundaries on my relationships with Catholics (to head off a "mixed marriage") as well as intense criticism and mockery of their tradition. As a boy, my theology really consisted of only one tenet: we are not Catholics. Then everything changed. Immersed in the Charismatic Renewal of the early 1970s, my father went through radical changes, but none more dramatic than his partnering with Father Murphy (from the Catholic parish down the street) to marry a Protestant to a Catholic when the need arose. "If they're in love, and they love the Lord, what's the difference?" Dad would ask, as if his previous position never existed. He and Father Murphy blended for the sake of the end user: the couple they were marrying. As beneficial as good teaching and effective judicatories can be, the grace for repentance on this scale is a work of the Holy Spirit, not application of a formula or a committee's agenda.

How Harmony Happens

Harmony begins with each brand's willingness to orient itself to the Lord in a way that affords maximum opportunity for the Spirit to administer the grace of God among us, blending our differences. Bringing any group of brands to a state of harmony means walking a path of repentance in several forms until reconciliation is achieved.

Commonality

Paul appealed for cessation of hostilities among the Corinthians and encouraged the Romans to build a unified culture, "so that with one heart and mouth you may glorify the God and Father of our Lord Jesus Christ."[23] The person of Christ and the mission of Christ stand at the center of the Church, two of the great common features defining the Christian community. When we treat these huge shared attributes as secondary because we prefer to criticize each other over issues such as social drinking, music style, or meat offered to idols, someone needs to repent. In New Testament terms, this repentance takes the form of preferring another's interests above my own for the sake of the faith community's witness to the world.[24]

The positive outcome for a repentant person or group takes the form of a focus on what really matters: who Jesus is and why He has called us. My friend Rod, the senior pastor of a congregation in the mid-South, says his large church features virtually every risk factor imaginable for interbrand warfare: contemporary worship in a conservative setting, traditional church folk side by side with college students, edgy young adult events next door to staid Sunday school classes. The key to the congregation's effectiveness is not unanimity or uniformity but mutual agreement on a common mission captured in the phrase "Every soul matters to God." Harmony at Rod's church grows out of a common mission sponsored by a common Lord (and judicious avoidance of incendiary situations). In the same way, the early Church found reconciliation over the issue of admitting Gentile Christians. Viewed from the perspective of their mission, no other choice seemed possible. As James pointed out conclusively, "The words of the prophets are in agreement with this."[25]

Conscience

Expecting brands to resemble each other defeats their purpose. The New Testament teaching on issues of conscience, or what Paul calls "disputable matters,"[26] plainly describes a large zone of flexible judgment outside the hard-truth issues of faith. That zone of judgment guarantees differences between individuals and groups who represent various brands. As the *body* of Christ, the Church reflects this diversity in the countless differences between the various parts, each of which desperately needs all the others.[27] Randy, a young adult pastor at Rod's church, recently took his group through a brand analysis, asking what the other brands in the church have contributed and what they have contributed to the others. His twentysomethings reached two conclusions: first, that they received many blessings from key individuals in the congregation to whom they returned very little; and second, that the church as a whole had adjusted to them, but they had done almost no adjusting to older people in the congregation. The group brainstormed ideas for investing time with and respect for older people to make the church feel like a real "family of believers."[28] One early idea commits each young adult to approach an older person before worship services and request to sit with them. Where years of sermons and meetings fail, harmony still grows from these simple gestures, at least for those who repent of the notion that differences are somehow outside of God's plan and embrace those differences as essential to appropriate blending.

Cultivation

Larry's fielding of complaints from self-appointed brand spokespersons in his region took a toll in hours and energy. Listening to him describe the dilemmas of leading a collection of combative subcultures led me to admire his courage and wisdom, but to conclude also that hard-liners on all sides receive a disproportionate amount of attention by virtue of their vehemence. Without a doubt, Larry's position carried the responsibility of dealing with complaints, a fact that dogmatic leaders knew how to exploit. The loudest voices, however, frequently represent a small minority within their particular brand. One survey, for example, found that the "worship wars" discussed endlessly by Christian congregational leaders in reality do not occur very often.[29] Focusing on them excessively raises the prospect of creating exactly what we fear.

Similarly, allowing hard-liner sentiment from any brand to command most of the attention within a group diminishes the contribution of the moderates who hold the potential for harmony in their hands. Repentance in this situation involves the decision to trust that, as the Lord told Paul when he was at risk in Corinth, "I have many people in this city."[30] I suspect that everywhere brand conflict breaks out, moderates in all the camps tend to get lost in the "fog of war," when exactly the opposite posture better serves the goal of harmony. Spiritual leaders give everyone a hearing but bolster the cause of reconciliation by proactively cultivating moderates (who are praying, with Jesus, for unity) rather than reacting to pressure from the margins. The raw material for harmony exists. I have met it. Good people are already in the city. We simply need to identify them, give them a chance to express their more conciliatory views, and create a venue in which collaborative relationships form. Harmony, then, grows from the middle out, not from the edges in. Over an eggs benedict breakfast, Rob, leading a large contemporary/experimental congregation in the upper Midwest, vented some dismay about the power of the traditionals in his denomination and the lack of progressive leaders with whom he could relate. He wants to stay connected to his fellowship, but not at the price of going it alone. He asked me who else was out there, and I was able to assure him that I know many others operating in his genre; they just haven't met each other yet.

In Rob's heart is not to stage a revolution but to grow a healthy center that can become a viable future for his church and his denomination. His ministry may well become the platform for a significant portion of that future.

Concentration

Grudging recognition of the contrast between brands falls far short of appreciating or even celebrating those dissimilarities. As in marriage, the choice of which of your spouse's traits to concentrate on determines whether peace or controversy characterizes the relationship. Every brand owns positives and negatives, so harmony calls for repenting of the tendency to highlight things we perceive as negative about those who think another way. One young friend recognized this tendency within himself and offered his confession to an e-group in these words:

> Here's my sin: I'm critical. Yup, I know you couldn't have guessed that one. But it's true—and I admit it. And I confess it. And I want to overcome it through God's help.
>
> I had a friend from seminary who attended an Ed Young conference on innovation. After returning, he said to me, "Ed Young really reminds me of you—without the cynicism." Every day, I understand more and more what he meant.
>
> I'm not sorry for being passionate or asking tough questions or pushing people to think in new ways. I'm sorry for not thinking redemptively. Everybody is a mixture of good and bad. And I get to choose which of those I will focus on. Most of the time, I choose poorly. And that is what I'm confessing.

If enough followers of Christ allowed the Spirit to deal with them in these terms, perhaps the positive features of others' brands would become much plainer, drawing our attention so as to forge appreciation where criticism used to live.

Contribution

Acceptance of difference and focus on the positive take concrete form as each brand begins to contribute from its strength to the whole body of Christ. Establishing harmony within a church, for example, means that traditionals bring their commitment to prayer and the Word, contemporaries bring their sense of excellence and pragmatism, and experimentals add energy and entrepreneurial risk taking. Randy's young adult ministry, for example, includes a half-dozen traditional couples (some of whom wear earplugs for the worship service) who simply mix in with the twentysomethings to offer them the love of spiritual grandparents. Watching Frank and Elaine, a retired couple, help prepare a sandwich buffet for a young adult lunch meeting felt as though we were about to gather around the Lord's table. In practical terms, financial support for the ministry comes in part from other brands within the congregation. Many parts, one body, but only if all decide to contribute to the mission from their strengths.

The off-road pathway of repentance offers the potential to attain a measure of harmony among brands. Taken cumulatively, these forms of repentance mean the members of all the brands bring their preferences to the cross, allowing anything that stands in the way of a common adoration of Christ and common devotion to His mission to die—the greater the death, the greater the new life. The more of our nonessentials we offer as a living sacrifice, the more our essentials occupy an appropriate position. No one is asked to change brands. None are asked to be what they are not. But everyone comes to the cross.

Chapter Nine

Reflection

The Discipline of Discernment

All of us own a theology, whether we realize it or not. Sitting in traffic proves this point conclusively, not in the form of opinion surveys but in the often more revealing medium of bumper stickers. "God, please deliver me from your followers!" pleads one, as the next driver addresses gender issues with: "My Goddess gave birth to your God" or "Eve was framed." A witch might proudly display, "Practice safe hex," while the car in the next lane advertises a Pentecostal church as the place "Where there's more than just talk." Another vehicle asks me to "Honk if you are God" and then presses for more: "Come the Rapture, can I have your car?" These tiny, mobile billboards also host more aggressive copy: "God was my copilot but we crashed in the mountains and I had to eat him," or, "Sorry I missed church. I've been studying witchcraft and becoming a lesbian." Eastern spirituality finds expression in stickers like "That was Zen. This is Tao," and Islam speaks to us at seventy miles per hour with "Man gets and forgets. Allah gives and forgives." Christian fundamentalists push back with slogans such as "Caution: Non-exposure to the Son will cause burning."

The average freeway hosts as many expressions of personal spirituality and religious affiliation as a small town. An online survey conducted by Beliefnet.com, for instance, asked site visitors to designate their favorite religious bumper stickers using a voting method of one, two, or three "honks."[1] Thousands participated, selecting as the winner a sticker that claimed to speak for God: "I don't question *your* existence." Runners up included, "Next time you think you're perfect . . . try walking on water"; "Lord, help me to be the person my dog thinks I am"; and the more traditional "America needs a faith lift." Though most exemplars of this art form seem to aim for humor ("It's OK, I didn't believe in reincarnation the last time either" or "Jesus is coming—look busy"), their sheer mass reflects more than just the American fascination with the automobile.

As incurably spiritual people, we theologize by nature. Even those of us who deny the existence of God have at least some informal ideas about His being and nature (or the supposed lack thereof). These ideas have many sources. I still have vivid memories of Miss Hanson, a tall, austere Swedish woman, literally putting the fear of God into my third grade Sunday school class by lecturing us from a wall poster of the Ten Commandments. During junior high school, Mr. Brehm, an older German man, made me memorize the Apostles' Creed to get passing marks in a Lutheran confirmation course. One weekday, he also walked our little group through the church's gloomy sanctuary, pointing out the symbolism of all the stained glass windows. The one depicting a swan piercing its own breast to feed starving chicks, he explained, spoke of Jesus' shedding His blood for us on the cross.

Christian theology logically seems like *our version* of the human tendency to make spirituality more specific and more portable, summing up everything discovered by the Church about God from the Bible and codifying it in tradition and doctrine. In fact, despite almost every conceivable challenge over many centuries, these biblical deductions culminate today in a rough but useful definition of orthodoxy among conservative Christians that helps to give shape to the life of the Church. That being said, however, my walk through the darkened sanctuary with Mr. Brehm taught me there is more at work here than logical deduction; there are also the swans. I needed the Ten Commandments, but I also needed to see the stained glass windows. To this day, I remember those windows more than most of the sermons I have heard or books I have read. They brought the Scriptures to life for a junior high school boy. Theology, then, is constructed by humans, and human beings are complex and contradictory, hopelessly complicating the idea of administering spirituality by deductive reasoning alone.

For example, the enormous public interest in a book and film such as *The Da Vinci Code* clearly demonstrates the residual significance of the Christian Scriptures in our culture, as well as the potential furor involved in tampering with the assumption of their authenticity or authority. Ironically, Rick Warren's *Purpose-Driven Life* captured the consumer market around the same time, tapping into an appetite for the practical wisdom from the Bible that might help us make sense of our lives. Our theology can be thought of as both a fixed *product* (core teachings that rarely change, scrutinized in *The Da Vinci Code*) and a fluid *process* (ongoing study probing the meaning and implications of the teachings, exemplified by the *Purpose-Driven Life*). This chapter defines *reflection* as the off-road spiritual discipline of thinking theologically in ways that enable us to listen to God, discerning how to root our lives and ministries in the person of Christ and the mission of God.

Theology and the Rest of Us

I am not a professional theologian. My formal exposure to the field consists of reading a few books, taking a couple of undergraduate courses (I remember a condescending religion professor looking over his glasses with pity at those of us who regarded the Bible as more than "literature"), and maybe three seminary classes—all beneficial. The point here is not to tell the story of theology with clinical accuracy but to depict, using the example of my own life and ministry, how the discipline seems to outsiders. I make no claim that my views are technically correct (even assuming the field itself agreed on what that looked like), just that they might be fairly representative of those of us who are the end users of theology. Since only a few thousand people actually make an academic profession of the subject, in the end professionals write theology and amateurs implement it. So here is how it looks to this amateur, and perhaps to you.

My first impression of theology was that it is the product of academic inquiry into the Scriptures by theologians, much as categorizing new species is the work of biologists exploring an Amazon rainforest. Thinking of theology only as product, however, seems to lend itself to a strictly *theory-and-practice* method. In other words, professional theologians armed with scholarly tools inaccessible to the rest of us define the teachings (theory) that the Church then implements (practices) in the real world. In this model, a theologian resembles a scientist doing basic research in hopes that someone one day turns those discoveries into a useful technology. The benefit of this approach is its capacity for investigating what we know about God without the potentially distorting influences (such as having to preach two brilliant sermons this coming Sunday) faced by pastors and other practitioners.

The currency of the theory-and-practice model displayed itself as I witnessed a debate over its assumptions between two friends, an academic theologian, Blaine, and a sociologist, Molly. Blaine contended earnestly that a theologian's background and personal context are irrelevant, since the discipline uses objective methods to study a fixed quantity, the Scriptures. Across the table, Molly, a veteran field researcher, rolled her eyes in a "You've just got to be kidding" way and responded with a question: "Blaine, you mean it would make no difference whether the person writing theology is a man or a woman?" He replied simply, "No. I don't believe it would." Sensing the impasse, Molly relinquished the option to lengthen a debate that would take us off the subject of our meeting; we proceeded, now with the logics of the theory-and-practice model and of its critics, in higher relief. Blaine sees himself almost as a scientist making observations to test hypotheses, while Molly cringes at what she sees as lack of self-awareness leading to the most powerful form of bias: the illusion of objectivity. As theologian John Stott concurs, "If we come to Scripture with our minds made up and closed, we will never hear the thunderclap of his Word. All we will hear is what we want to hear, the soothing echoes of our own *cultural prejudice*."[2]

In *A Primer on Postmodernism,* the late theologian Stanley Grenz illustrates this great divide by cautioning his readers that "I am not in a position to specify precisely how Christians should engage in ministry to the postmodern generations. I am, after all, an academic. I leave to seasoned practitioners—like you—the task of moving from an understanding of, to ministry to, the *Star Trek* generation."[3]

This humble statement displays the practical limitations of product theology without forsaking its great strength, the ability to draw the Church's attention to the biblical basis for our relationship of obedience to God and love for humanity. This informal scholarly consensus approximates a critical mass of key definitions about the faith and discourages followers of Christ from looking into the Bible, in James's words, like the person "who looks at his face in a mirror and, after looking at himself, goes away and immediately forgets what he looks like."[4]

Evangelicals tend to see only orthodoxy at stake here, but the nature of theology itself also is in play. As Dean Timothy George of the Beeson Divinity School points out, "Theologians are not freelance scholars of religion, but trustees of the deposit of faith that they, like pastors, are charged with passing on intact to the rising generation."[5] In a strict theory-and-practice model, assumptions like Blaine's (the relative unimportance of context) carry the risk of detaching a discipline that we need desperately from the life of the church it should serve, reducing the enterprise to a disembodied discussion among a closed circle of professors and students.

Clearly, an extreme form of the theory-and-practice dichotomy (and not all forms are extreme) offers an inadequate foundation for the life of the Church in a post-Christendom context. In fact, we might ask if the great gulf fixed between ideas and mission contributed to putting us into a post-Christendom era.

In my second take on theology, I concluded that in response to the tensions created by the product orientation the field turns to the *process* side for relief, atomizing into a huge variety of context-driven (as with Latin American theology) and theory-driven (for example, postmodern theology) subdisciplines. Although conservative theory-and-practice specialists view the text as a given, often exploring it with an historical-critical lens, process scholars tend to understand the method as the given and the text as assuming meaning depending on the interpreter. These studies command great interest in the academic community, but their significance to the Church depends, as with the theory-and-practice model, on adoption of their interpretive method, making them largely inaccessible outside the scholarly setting. Duke University emeritus religion professor Robert Osborn laments, "In my world, it is no longer clear what theology is, where it can or should be done, or how."[6]

The real focus in the clash of product and process involves much more than defining orthodoxy, or a struggle between reformers and traditionalists.[7] How we live out our theology and make it comprehensible to society holds a central place in the discussion. When the Father wanted to reveal Himself to the world, He sent His Son Jesus as the Word made flesh, to *be* the truth and *live* the truth before our eyes.[8] Making our theology alive today requires the same ability to incarnate truth rooted in the discipline of *reflecting* on God's work so that we can discern God's voice, rather than relying only on knowing theologies (which is valuable in other ways). McGill University theology professor Douglas John Hall suggests an example with these rhetorical questions:

> What would it mean to go to the Scriptures (e.g., to the Pauline metaphor of the body and its many members) with such contemporary experiences and questions fully present and articulated—not the familiar questions of generations of theological classrooms, but concrete questions, posed by the lives we know and honed into graphic forms by the best of our novelists, filmmakers, and social commentators? And would a congregation whose life and work were informed by such a meeting of text and context be satisfied, then, with the kind of community gathered for worship on Sunday mornings in towns and cities throughout North America, or at coffee hours after worship?[9]

Hall contends that bringing "text and context" together pragmatically would make it difficult for at least some of our ministry forms to stay as they are.

Much of the current interest in theology in film, for example, seems to have this issue at heart. How do we think of Pentecostal worship after seeing Robert Duvall's *The Apostle*? What if a drama such as *Kingdom of Heaven* or a comedy such as *Saved* motivated reexamination of how we appear to the sought in culture? The point here is not that doctrine should be molded to images crafted in Hollywood but that appropriate contact with a broader context might jar us from the complacency of assuming that our current ministry defines the limit of what God is willing to do.

Theological Reflection

In taking the theory-practice divide too seriously, some unreflective practitioners (and their followers) consider theology a synonym for doctrine and simply assume that possessing the latter makes any further understanding of the former a waste of time. As a consequence, the Church tends to be served either by philosophers or plumbers, or what David Livermore refers to in the context of youth ministry education as the struggle of "irrelevant theorists vs. mindless practitioners,"[10] two clans that communicate little and seldom get along—but that have much in common! Leaders who undervalue reflection risk underdeveloping their capacity for discerning what God is up to in their midst, trapping themselves in a cold pragmatism that resonates too much with the world around us and for which theological terminology serves little more than a cosmetic purpose. In this context, evangelism may mean little more than marketing, salvation becomes a response card turned in at the Christmas concert, and discipleship reduces to a certificate verifying that one has filled in all the blanks necessary to complete a certain class. One participant in a doctoral class, for instance—obviously fuming over my material on reflection and the interior life—burst out cathartically, "*Now* you're helping me!" when I offered a brief comment on how to organize pastoral teams. His mania for solutions to problems of mechanics amounted to a convenient diversion from the solution he needed for his own life. From the student's perspective, as New Testament scholar Peter Nelson puts it, "If you can't graph positive results, what is the point?"[11] Devoted to the quest for outcomes, these über-pragmatists struggle to understand that the "point" is Christ Himself.

Practitioners without reflective disciplines tend to invest their ministry only in certain important, but ultimately secondary, questions:

- *What?* The issue of *genre* addresses the ministry's format (for example, singles ministry, prayer group, and so on).
- *Where?* Location concerns not just the geography of ministry but the *calling* to a particular group of people.
- *How?* This most compelling question of *mechanics* deals with growing the ministry and often consumes virtually all of a leader's time.
- *When?* The significance of *scheduling* grows every day in our frenetically busy culture (an alternative service on Saturday night, or Sunday night, or both?).
- *How many?* The question of *results* often reduces to attendance and budget growth amplified by a few anecdotes illustrating success.

As important as these concerns are for the execution of ministry, they engage leaders in a style that looks remarkably like the way the world runs organizations.

My seminary's president, Byron Klaus, refers to this tendency as "hyper-pragmatism" and challenges those who lead this way with the stark reality of Jesus' teaching on the ultimate evaluation of our efforts.[12] The final question is not the extent of *our* involvement but the extent of *His* involvement. Theological reflection, then, begins with prioritizing two questions, focusing on them both before and while handling other ministry issues:

- *Why?* The issue of *mission* represents the critical factor. Does the ministry really prepare us to co-labor with Christ, being sent as the Father sent Him, or only to tweak up our mechanics to attract a larger crowd? Too often, the level of execution required to drive the numbers consumes almost all of the leader's energy. In the play-book ministries of Christendom, supported by a church-going culture, this technique actually worked much of the time. However, today's audience resembles a moving target, meaning that one of our primary tasks is fundamentally theological: keeping the ministry accountable to the mission. The purpose of theology is therefore to support the Church in cooperating with the mission of God, not the other way around.

- *Who?* The answer to this question is God, who surpasses everything else as our primary calling. The person of Christ must be the center of everything, and His Spirit the instigator and power for all forms of ministry. If pursuit of Christian activities fails to result in a greater personal relationship with Christ, we miss the point and need to ask if our ministry represents Christian leadership or just Christians leading, or just leading Christians. Again, the product of theology occupies an essential position, requiring that the question of who God is and what He wants be answered at every turn. Reflection on God's activity among us places leaders in the proper posture for listening to God's voice as the source of direction in ministry, and waiting for God's Spirit to empower us in the task. Mechanics become important (which they are) only as they form a response to God's leading.

Theological reflection recognizes that all of these questions serve us well only when put in proper priority. Out of theological order, we become indistinguishable from the world in our methods, regarding praxis as separate from doctrine and experience, rendering spiritual things largely irrelevant to the practical arts that (wink, nod) actually get the job done. In this sense, the plumbers own just as much responsibility for firewalling theory from practice as do the philosophers, each group creating the divide to defend its own identity and expand its own power. The world around us sees the disconnect.

Theological reflection offers a way to integrate the virtues of both the product and the process approaches so that theology serves the mission of the Church in practical, but faithful, terms. There are many available perspectives on this model, but the key premise assumes that experience serves not as a substitute but as a stimulus to theology. As Christ puts all teaching in human form, bringing it into our experience, theological reflection helps leaders put theology into a living form by providing the off-road discipline of discerning God's voice at the sidewalk level. The culture around us poses questions that may well be God challenging the Church with opportunities to make biblical truth concrete for the world. The book of Acts, for example, offers at least nine recorded instances of apostolic preaching taking place in response to questions (direct or implied) from the outside.[13] Some of these inquiries represent accusations or interrogations, but the principle remains that at least some of the Church's preaching ministry *responded* to the spiritual dynamics of the culture, beginning with the crowd of people present on the Day of Pentecost who asked one another, "What does this mean?"[14] Peter interprets this query as God opening a door to speak to the assembled crowd. The first recorded public statement of apostolic teaching takes place not in a seminary but in response to the curiosity of a throng meeting in the street. This is theology's natural home.

Christian leaders today need to listen for the questions posed by those navigating our cultural perfect storm, regardless of the relationship of those voices to the Church. This sort of humility requires no compromise of orthodoxy but goes a long way toward defusing an often suspicious post-Christian audience, while maturing the Church in its devotion to Christ.

Theological reflection, then, is the art of responding theologically to life and ministry because God is active in both, affording the opportunity for God to speak to us in ways that can shape our perspective on ourselves and our ministry. Reflection and discernment lead to more ministry and in turn to more theologizing, producing a cycle of reflective living. Two simple diagrams can clarify the distinction between the theory-and-practice and theological-reflection models.

The simple reflective process depicted here features multiple starting points and only supplements the product theologies that furnish its raw material by connecting them to the Church in a life-giving way. But theological reflection also involves a process over time that is based on a certain method of discernment, a way of seeking God's interpretation of our life experience, rather than a block of theological content. This approach obviously calls for a level of gracious and mature dialogue. One example looks like this:[15]

- *We attempt to cooperate with God in ministry.* Being on mission with Jesus affords infinite opportunities to engage in ministry, sometimes in ways that are especially meaningful, perhaps even rising to the status of a critical incident. For example, let's say that after reading a few books on the subject your ministry plans a Celtic-style worship service targeting postmoderns—and it fails miserably.
- *We process the event.* "Success" does not make me spiritual any more than failure makes me unholy. An event calls for a season of personal and corporate processing, a time of reflective thought that results in a written debriefing of the experience. The purpose of

Theory-Practice

Theological reflection

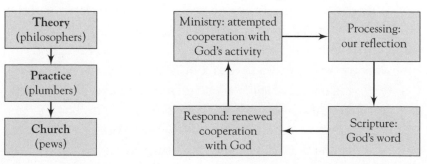

the exercise is to create white space in which God has a chance to speak to us about our best efforts—whether they succeeded or failed. The debrief process is most effective when shared among the members of a ministry team, church leadership circle, or other group, with each member capturing impressions in writing. The core of this season is brutal honesty about what we have experienced, how it made us feel, and where things went right or wrong. In the case of our example, the group debriefs on the initial failure (defined by very low attendance) of the Celtic outreach service for postmodern.

• *We use Scripture as a mirror.* Once written debriefs have been created, shared, and discussed, participants spend some time meditating on the experience, praying with each other, and listening for God's direction in key Scriptures. Finding passages that bear importantly on the event, leaders brainstorm the relationship between what God says through the Word and their own response to the event, all the time asking the Spirit to speak to them as individuals and as a group. The group then reviews its written debriefs in light of the Scriptures selected and prays through the issue of how their perspectives change by interaction with the Word, looking out for their own cultural prejudices, false assumptions, and ungodly attitudes as well as the positive aspects of the event. To continue our example, perhaps the leadership team discerns, among other things, that the postmodern event was created in a spirit of competition with a nearby congregation that is receiving notoriety for creating a nontraditional young adult service. Recognizing the deficiencies in both the motivation and the results could lead to revisiting the theology of the church until it represents something truly missional to which the group pledges to hold itself accountable. Ultimately the group must ask, "What is God saying to us, and what are we prepared to do about that?"

• *We respond in renewed cooperation with God.* The discernments from these stages can be used to form the next phase of your ministry's growth. Ask exactly how things will be done in greater obedience to the Spirit's voice the next time. Chances are you will find the *why* and *who* questions now becoming a priority in your thinking. If these issues occupy the core of your discussion, many of the other questions become easier. Just as important, at this point, ask how *you need to change* as leaders in order to better represent the love of Christ, and to do ministry in His name. Concluding our example, your leadership team may discern that the next step is to humble themselves, spending time with the citizens of emerging culture rather than scheduling events based on principles culled from popular books.

This sort of spirit, tearing down the theory-practice divide, itself is a positive witness, depicting Christianity as a spiritual life that makes sense because it is lived in obedience to God, and so generates missional living, regardless of how the pragmatic questions play out ultimately. Our increasingly post-Christendom context affords an important opportunity to energize theology with more missional and Christo-centric dynamics, and to humble the Church so that we become more suitable "jars of clay" to hold the "treasure" of the gospel.[16]

A Theology Worth Smuggling

Sheathed in cheap, dark wood paneling, the pastor's study in which we held our board meetings looked like a leftover from the 1960s. In a discussion one night, we began to talk about how to help people in our church grow spiritually. Taking a marker in hand, I stood up, walked to the long white strip of paper taped to the wall, and asked the board members, "Who do we know in our church that, to the eye, is growing spiritually?" Warming to the question, in just a minute or two we listed the names of about ten people plainly thriving on the grace of God, becoming someone they had never met before. I still recall that conversation as the most joyful moment of leading the group.

The next question presented more difficulty: "What, if anything, do these growing people have in common?" In silence, we all ran our eyes over the paper on the wall looking for clues. As we began to talk through what we knew about these friends, a common element surfaced: every single one of these people somehow found his or her way into an informal network of nurturing relationships.

I took a deep breath and asked the third question: "What could we do to make sure that everyone in our church has this kind of experience?" Now it got really quiet. We enjoyed listing the growing people and thinking about their traits. Both gave us the feeling that perhaps we were doing a few things right. But trying to systematize the experience of our people stopped us dead in our tracks.

Of course, the obvious answers beckoned. Just start cell groups! Roll out more traditional Sunday school classes! Disperse the congregation into postmodern house churches! But in our context, these fine ideas collided with the reality that our growing people had *spontaneously* found their way into *informal* networks that required minimal administrative support. In other words, all the good stuff happened in the cracks between our complicated programs. Our discussion that night led us to the question of how God was at work among us, and what God's activity implied for our own. Followed to its logical conclusion, this stream of discernment (relationships, spontaneity, groups) would have led to a complete retooling of our church's very traditional structure.

The ability to reflect theologically can represent the difference between thirty years of experience in ministry and three years of experience repeated ten times. Prioritizing the *why* and *who* questions offers a first step toward this reflective discipline, with the practical benefit of being a vehicle for living theologically. As pastoral theologian Robert L. Kinast notes: "Theological reflection is . . . not satisfied with learning more about God but asks the person to consider what difference God's presence makes (the reflection stage) and what God expects as a result (the action stage). This integration of reflection and action is ultimately what makes theological reflection theological."[17] Leaders who view ministry in this synthetic way defy easy categorization; they choose to live in the unyielding tension between blue-sky theory and let's-get-on-with-the-show pragmatism, sometimes enduring criticism from both sides.

I think of these leaders as practical theologians.[18] Not as the opposite of impractical theologians, for the developers of ideas lacking real-world implications engage more in philosophy about God than in theology proper. Conversely, programming without theological reflectivity is not fully *ministry* either, but more a form of brute action. Both enterprises could be undertaken by well-meaning atheists. This ironic common ground forms a strange bond between those at either extreme of the divide, making them easy to identify.

A synthesis (not a balance) of idea and initiative, of construct and commitment requires living faith in Jesus Christ. Both of the extremes, academic and pragmatic, can be emulated by anyone who has the interest and the intelligence. The academic approach risks spending a lifetime guarding what someone has called "the cutting edge of irrelevance."[19] The pragmatic flirts with an expediency that produces widely admired forms of success in which Christ's role is secondary to our own. But the synthesis, what my seminary calls "knowledge on fire," or what Klaus refers to as "theological thoroughness," is so daunting as to cultivate dependence on the person of Christ, who came as God's synthesis of Word and flesh, and a love for the Church and the world, which is the reason He came. Timothy George draws this example from the life of a Harvard scholar:

> When Harvey Cox was a student minister in Berlin in 1962, one year after the erection of the Wall, he was able to travel back and forth between East and West because he held an American passport. He thus became a courier for pastors and Christian laypeople on both sides of that divide and was sometimes able to smuggle theological books into the East. What the people wanted most were copies of Barth's *Church Dogmatics*. "To carry in something by Bultmann would have been a wasted risk," Cox said. "Let the Bourgeois preachers in West Germany agonize about the disappearance of the

three-decker universe and existentialism. We had weightier matters to confront." This is a parable for us today. A theology more enamored with novelty than fidelity is not worth smuggling, for it will not nourish the mission of the church nor build up the people of God.[20]

A theology not worth smuggling is not worth having. Becoming a practical theologian means drawing from the very best of theological product, but doing so connected to the life of the Church by theological process. A theology worth smuggling serves the Church well because it is based on listening to God rather than just talking and writing about God—the kind of reflection that cultivates intimacy with Christ, the core of the missional life.

Chapter Ten

Opportunity

The Discipline of Making Room

In need of some R&R and a new pair of sunglasses, we were really looking forward to our tour of Pearl Street in the heart of Boulder, Colorado. Brad and Julie, church planters in the city, directed us there and guided our walking tour of this cobblestone area sealed off from vehicular traffic and reserved just for people like us. Sunglasses were no problem since there were kiosks packed with knock-offs of every brand on every block, forming a gauntlet designed to filter money from tourists. The shops, restaurants, and book stores formed a city-within-the-city, accentuated by street entertainers ranging from jugglers to contortionists, one of whom stuffed himself into a two-foot Plexiglas cube just to hold a crowd.

Interestingly enough, the circuslike atmosphere also had an undercurrent of spirituality running through it. Stores devoted to every form of mysticism (especially anything Tibetan) stood out among the many retail outlets. Visiting one of them, we found a plastic case (about the size of the cube into which the contortionist folded himself) in the center of the store prominently displaying magic wands. The wands, however, came complete with a small disclaimer placard assuring customers that they posed no health hazard, having been officially deactivated. A little later, outside on the brick promenade, we walked past a woman who I assumed was leaning against a tree for a moment's respite, only to realize she had the tree in a full bear hug. I surmised the woman-tree relationship involved something of great spiritual significance to her (an exchange of energy fields?) but of unknown significance to the tree.

Compound spiritualities make up Boulder's religion the way mountainous terrain shapes its aesthetic, and the University of Colorado influences its intellectual life. Guarded by a two-mile green belt and a one-way-in, one-way-out road system, the city stands as a beacon of enlightened living in the foothills of the Rockies. Life appears so fine in Boulder that panhandlers flock there for the good treatment they receive, and even the homeless shelter wins national awards for quality. Witnessing what seemed like a microcosm of Sweden right here in America, populated by what Ravi Zacharias has called "happy thinking pagans,"[1] I started thinking about whether the city's misery quotient reaches the threshold for conventional evangelism to make sense. Church planting in a parallel situation in the Pacific Northwest, my friend Bill put it bluntly: "My people *have* no felt needs."

After one particularly extraordinary salad eaten in the brilliant mountain sunshine next to a rushing stream, I asked Brad, "How do you reach people in a place like this, a place that's just . . . well . . . perfect?" We pondered the issue for a while, walking the streets and reflecting on the population's affluence, liberal politics, mania for recreation, and supreme commitment to zero growth (that is, no Wal-Marts) in Boulder. The joy of lunching in bustling outdoor cafes and drinking great coffee in funky bookstores only reinforced the question: What does Jesus offer to the person leaving her office at the university, driving her Volvo to a Wiccan ceremony, and then on to a discussion group on the Latin American novel? The discomfort of thinking this issue through surfaced how much I sometimes rely on emergency, crises, or just general wretchedness to open the door for mission (as opposed to alleviating suffering just because it's right). It makes me see what a handy substitute it is for living a witness before people I actually know, with whom I have something very personal at stake. Without a doubt, touching human need represents Christ well, but the needs in this town concealed themselves behind smiling faces, GORE-TEX, vanilla lattes, and hybrid SUVs.

I gave Brad a summary of my thoughts sometime during the second day in town: "The first question you'll have to answer is, 'What could possibly be better than Boulder?' " The town represented, at least on the surface, a virtual humanist paradise, one of the cleanest, safest, healthiest, fairest environments ever developed within the reach of upper-middle-class Anglos. In fact, some locals viewed Colorado Springs as their evil twin, the headquarters of conservative Christian organizations all dedicated to demolishing everything Boulder stands for by creating something like a fundamentalist evangelical theocracy. Brad and Julie realized that, with the slightest provocation, these stereotypes would be applied just as well to them in the minds of most locals. We concluded that, without a ministry in the power of the Holy Spirit, Christian mission in the city was doomed to being buried alive in the Boulder lifestyle, becoming just one more niche on Pearl Street.

This chapter extends the personal off-road discipline of witness to the group level, arguing for the spiritual discipline of making room for God, so that the people of Boulder experience an environment where the Holy Spirit can invite them into a relationship with Christ. This *spatial* model assumes that all of life holds the potential to form these environments, and that every follower of Christ can participate in them. Ironically, the worship services that churched people sometimes count on to reach the unchurched may offer precious little real opportunity for this to happen.[2] Services take on a missional dimension when they reflect individual lives serving as vehicles for the Spirit to invite people into an exploration of Jesus' identity and work. The benefits for missional people are considerable. Writing in the context of the Externally Focused Church, Eric Swanson notes: "Lives are most likely to be changed when people engage with people. People feel their worth only when they are affirmed by other people. Good deeds can be done from afar, but good news can only be shared up close. Love is a shared experience. . . . As we engage with other people, God may use us to change the ending of their story."[3] They may also change the ending of ours.

Uncivil Wars

Jesus' instructions to go into all the world and make disciples seem so direct, so simple, until we try to translate them into the terms of daily life. Students of the Church estimate that approximately 250 plans to evangelize the world were proposed by 1900, with another 1,150 or so added during the twentieth century, many of them coalescing around the end of the last millennium, with none of them succeeding.[4] But these initiatives, for all the good they accomplished, seem to leave much of the planet untouched, especially Western Europe and portions of the United States. Perhaps we expect global strategies to take on challenges that individual followers of Christ seldom engage except, in Presbyterian pastor Eli Morris's terms, by contributing "money and things," or time to "engage in projects."[5] Both kinds of effort merit praise, of course, but both are also limited to the impersonal (mailing a check) or the institutional (refurbishing classrooms) levels only.

Getting personal about mission means punching through several difficult dilemmas that stand in the way of our efforts. The first involves the theological question of *why* the Seeker looks for the sought so diligently. From one perspective, the sought enter the Kingdom of God because of the Seeker's decision before time began, with the Church serving mainly as the stage on which this script plays itself out. However, other theologians of good will and equal qualification hold that the sought exercise at least a measure of choice over their connection to the Seeker, often protesting the fairness of the scripted model and claiming that it deprives life of meaning by reducing humans to God's slaves rather than God's children. Script advocates respond by claiming that they merely reflect the logic of the Scriptures inspired by a sovereign God, and that free will theory engenders more unfairness by permitting me to doom my neighbor for eternity by forgetting the lunch appointment that would have been our last chance to talk about Christ. Neither of these options seems particularly mission-friendly.

The second dilemma resides on the organizational level, where followers of Jesus debate *how* the Church serves to connect the sought to the Seeker. Those trusting in highly intentional approaches to congregational life that emphasize strategy-driven models and organized ministries argue that the leadership arts applied to Christian organizations will yield optimal results. Their case generally rests on citing several large congregations as high-profile examples of the kind of success possible when insightful strategy and deliberate processes guide ministry. Advocates of inspirational models protest that adopting business-style methods means adopting the values of secular culture, leaving no white space for God to move in. Sovereign interventions by the Spirit displaying the power of God represent the method of the early Church, they claim, pointing to the absence of a five-year strategic plan in the New Testament.

The intentional camp contends that the Church enjoys legitimate access to any method not contradicting the Scriptures and proven effective in the real world. Inspirationalists react in dismay to such claims, preaching that the Church must avoid any method not endorsed by biblical precept or example, regardless of the so-called success earned in a business context.

These debates seldom find resolution because neither side will examine its assumptions or admit the exceptions to its claims. For example, intentionalists often hesitate to disclose the back stories on their high-profile case studies, overlooking the special conditions or advantages (such as financial backing, core leadership reaped from the implosion of a neighboring church, a supremely talented leader) they enjoy that are inapplicable to virtually any other situation. Inspirationalists commit the same fallacy in reverse, whenever exaggerated claims or exaggerated lifestyles produce questionable credibility in ministry. A fair-minded person would be right to ask if this fault line running through the Church makes any sense. Does anyone *really* want powerless planning, or planless power? When considered in these terms, the debate sounds more like a civil war over ministry culture than a search for God's mind on evangelism. I am unaware of any sought person coming to faith in such a discussion.

In truth, enough successes and failures exist in all the camps to invalidate any claim of an exclusive right to God's approval in principle, or effectiveness in practice. From many years of church research, in fact, I would say the lack of connection between any particular congregational model and predictable effectiveness represents the one thing we may actually know for sure. There are no formulas. Yet the American Church lives with constant pressure to reduce mission to evangelism, and then reduce evangelism to either strategy or experience alone. Consider how these approaches would work (and they sometimes do) for one young man who describes his spiritual journey in these terms: "I came to realize that the search of the philosophers for a grand scheme that would encompass everything was illusory. Only a theism that combined God with equal measures of truth, love, and justice could do the trick. But since I could not imagine myself being religious, and had indeed become more raucously secular, I did not consider that to be an option for me."[6]

Stanford philosopher Richard Rorty, one of the leading voices in secular pragmatic philosophy, searched as a younger man not for a way to "get saved" but for some means of understanding the whole universe in spiritual terms—a unified field theory of the soul.

I find it difficult to believe that any faction in the uncivil wars so endemic to Christianity offers much that Rorty might find of interest. If mission is portrayed as either the product of human engineering or the sovereign intervention of God, the former often looks like a program, with budgets and ID badges, while the latter sounds a lot like a tent meeting. Both approaches have their place, but in isolation neither is likely to be sufficient in a culture that tends to view programs as cynical marketing ploys and crowds as the raw material of manipulation. Like Rorty, the citizen of post-Christendom looks for insight into ever-larger questions that sometimes exceed the scope of our answers.

Spatial Evangelism

The practice of evangelism involves making room for the Spirit to draw the sought into a saving encounter with the Seeker through Christ. The Church's job is not to save people but to shape the space in which God calls them to Himself. So I propose that, in addition to other perspectives, we start thinking of evangelism three-dimensionally, as a volume of missional space, perhaps like the plastic cube into which the lanky contortionist on that Boulder street corner tried to jam himself. The difference is that missional space has flexible but connected dimensions such as heart, Spirit, and venue. The contortionist, like some ministries, works with a fixed volume and struggles to fit within it, while missional leaders search constantly for ways to make their operating space larger and better suited to their context.

The point here is not the shape of the cube but the concept of evangelism as the ministry of expanding the volume in which the Spirit invites the sought to meet Jesus. Those engaged in uncivil wars think in the geometry of two dimensions, one being the Church and the other being the sought (or the lost, the pagan, the seeker, the pre-Christian, the post-Christian, and so forth). Two points define a line, but not a volume. Similarly, easy dichotomics fail to

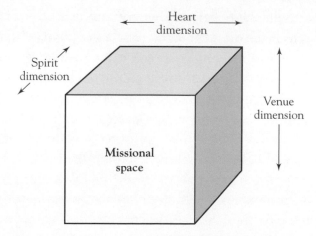

open up the third dimension of the Spirit, the dimension that shapes the environment into which the unregenerate heart finds eternal life through a redeeming relationship with the living Christ. As an example, think of spatial evangelism as defined by dimensions like the three discussed here.

The Heart Dimension

Hearts closed and defensive toward the sought abound, with an attitude that deflates the space in which the Spirit might have operated among them. Led by John, for example, some of Jesus' hard-hearted disciples tried to prohibit a man without membership in their exclusive club of twelve from using the Lord's name to cast out demons. James and John then asked Jesus for permission to call down destruction on the Samaritan villages that refused His presence. In both cases, self-righteousness trumped love. No wonder Jesus paused to teach the twelve about inclusion, delivering a stinging rebuke for their readiness to destroy the very people He intended to teach, heal, and save. Luke's account of these two incidents concludes with a cryptic comment: "and they went to another village."[7] Jesus refused to allow the lovelessness of His closest followers to delay His mission to the next village, or to the world; He pushed on, and so should we.

Nevertheless, this active variety of lovelessness pales in comparison to its much more common, passive counterpart. In response to a question about whom we should call neighbor, Jesus told of a man robbed, beaten, and left to die on the road to Jericho. A priest and a Levite passed him by on the other side, but a Samaritan "took pity on him" and rendered extraordinary aid to this victim of violent crime, even ensuring his long-term care and becoming the only true neighbor to the man left beside the road. Jesus' interrogator probably assumed that the story's moral would be some definition of the group who held neighbor status. But Jesus answered a better question than the man asked, pointing out that neighborliness is an action, not a status.

This familiar parable speaks to the danger of feeling justified because one's relationships leave others no worse off than when one found them. I feel this danger every time I drive past my neighbors' house without stopping to inquire about their health, see their new baby, or just generally make friends. No overt harm is done, but no love is shared either.

The scale of our love serves as a limiting factor on the dimensions of our missional space because it determines the size and depth of our relationships with the sought. As theologian Lesslie Newbigin points out, we have few other options:

> How is it possible that the gospel should be credible, that people should come to believe that the power which has the last word on human affairs is represented by a man hanging on a cross? I am suggesting that the only answer, the only hermeneutic of the gospel, is a congregation of men and women who believe it and live it. . . . Evangelistic campaigns, distribution of Bibles and Christian literature, conferences, and even books such as this one . . . are all secondary, and . . . they have power to accomplish their purpose only as they are rooted in and lead back to a believing community. Jesus . . . *did not write a book but formed a community.*[8]

Without love, the other dimensions collapse into meaninglessness, regardless of method or theology, becoming more of "a resounding gong or a clanging cymbal"[9] than the voice of the Seeker.

In several years of field observation, for example, I have met too many emerging ministry leaders who (in Thomas Hohstadt's words) "are making the same mistake the Boomers made: They are turning their culture into a religion," almost guaranteeing a younger version of the uncivil wars already too common in the Church.[10] Embracing culture and loving the ministry are not enough. Mission begins in feeling the Seeker's love for the sought poured "into our hearts by the Holy Spirit, whom he has given us."[11] My friend Matt taught me a valuable lesson on this point one day in my office while discussing his plans for church planting in Boulder.

When I asked about his fit with the community, he replied, "I *like* liberals!" and went on to describe his enjoyment of spending time with "blue state" citizens. He did not just love them out of obligation; he *liked* them, liked drinking coffee with them, liked getting to know them, liked them enough to buy a hybrid SUV just to fit in. Like catalyzes love, and love grows the capacity for mission in every form.

The Venue Dimension

Love needs an address. Without a specific location, it remains an abstract idea or a sentimental impulse, the kind of love on which pop music lyrics obsess. Relationship presents the site where love makes a home, but these bonds require some location in which to happen. Missional living means connecting with the sought in specific places, so that the Seeker expresses His love through us in specific ways. Of course, church services offer one such place, and when created from a missional heart they impose no stumbling block to the sought other than Christ Himself. But the sought sometimes question the need to attend such an event to find a God who seems so available otherwise. Deterred by institutions but drawn to the search for answers in other forms, they access relationships in forms outside of Sunday morning—such as the Internet.

   Cyberspace. Bill Easum compares the influence today's Internet has on evangelism to the fifty-thousand-mile Roman road system that allowed the apostles to preach throughout the empire, and the reformer's use of the printing press in the Renaissance to put Bibles and pamphlets in the hands of the common person.[12] Almost two-thirds of American Internet users have already gone online for religious or spiritual purposes.[13] With the number of teenagers online now approaching fifty million, the potential impact of Internet spirituality on future generations defies prediction.

But the Internet is *not* just a communication network; it is a *culture* all its own. (It helps me to think of it as the eighth continent.) So a billboard-style, "this is when we meet" site seldom serves outsiders well because they expect to find a destination, an address at which real relationship and spiritual research (perhaps combined) happen in one click. If a site fails to facilitate some kind of connection while answering questions no one is asking, it represents a waste of electrons. The primary fault of most Christian Websites springs from their overwhelmingly one-way communication pattern. Most of the time, clicking on an e-mail link or logging into a discussion board constitute the only options for talking back, often appearing more like exceptions in a site devoted to promoting a ministry. What would happen if this monologue approach were reversed and sites were designed to answer the question, "How could the sought best develop a relationship with our faith community?"

Third Place. In *The Great Good Place*, Ray Oldenburg contrasts our homes and workplaces with another realm: "The *third place* is a generic designation for a great variety of public places that host the regular, voluntary, informal, and happily anticipated gatherings of individuals beyond the realms of home and work."[14] The most common incarnation of the third-place principle in evangelism today may be the Christian coffee house, which aims to be a place where the sought can feel God and meet credible Christians on neutral turf. The best ministries of this sort that I have visited emphasize passive witness. J. D. and Jen Bump, for example, operated a shop actually called the Third Place, located on "the strip," a street full of bars near the campus of Oklahoma State University. Twelve hundred people, mainly the sought, came through their doors weekly, some of whom found their way next door to the University Worship Center. Today, they do the same in Europe while our mutual friend Nick continues the Third Place, now on the other side of the church.

Other friends create third places in art galleries (Scott and Tiffany) or community centers (Tony and Hannah). Regardless of whether the space is virtual or physical, love needs a place where relationship develops in order to take a concrete form. Jesus came to earth, rather than dictating teaching or performing miracles from heaven. He sought us out and offered us relationship by coming to a specific place and time according to the purposes of the Father. The absence of a relationship dimension renders love almost null and void by depriving it of a context in which to be lived out with the sought. The easiest examples here pertain to a congregation baffled by its lack of evangelistic effectiveness while never thinking to question the level of resources committed to this purpose, or a person who longs to connect with the sought but never builds friendships for their own sake. In both cases love overflows, but without a place to assume some practical influence in someone else's life it may produce little more than guilty Christians.

The Spirit Dimension

Caring profoundly about the sought and developing venues in which to interact with them creates only the potential for mission. Nothing else happens without the agency and power of the Holy Spirit. Jesus felt so strongly about this necessity that He actually commanded His disciples to stay in Jerusalem until "you have been clothed with power from on high,"[15] promising them that the Spirit's power would carry their witness to the whole planet. A local Jewish sect explodes into a regional and then a global force under the influence of the same Spirit who raised Jesus from the dead. In other words, although Christian mission requires a commitment of both our heart and our relationship venues, reducing it to these elements renders mission two-dimensional (2D), comparable to a marketing plan about which we care deeply.

Attempting to live the mission in these terms deprives Christ's followers of their greatest opportunity for spiritual growth and appears artificial to the sought. Sarah, a gen X church visitor, describes her reaction to 2D mission:

We know you have tried to get us to church. That's part of the problem. Many of your appeals have been carefully calculated for success and that turns our collective stomach. Take worship, for instance: you think that fashionably cutting-edge liturgies relate to us on our level, but the fact is, we can find better entertainment elsewhere. The same goes for anything you term "contemporary." We see right through it. It is up to date for the sake of being up to date, and we are not impressed by the results.[16]

Ironically, Sarah seems more discerning of shortcomings in mission than the members of the sort of congregation to which she refers. Someone cared enough to create a "cutting-edge liturgy" to attract her, but the absence of something else led her to understand the venue as a contrivance, a sort of gospel infomercial pitched to the sought.

On a larger scale, Sarah's thinking reminds me of the temporary spike in church attendance in the weeks following September 11, 2001. Survey data indicate that a return to the baseline happened in just about a month, with little residual effect on the population as a whole.[17] I have always wondered: What *did not happen* in those thirty days or so that would have attracted the sought to the Seeker in our churches? Pastors frequently complain about low attendance, assuming that if people just tried one of the services or small groups the experience would convert them into members. In fact, for some pastors this goal almost summarizes the mission of Jesus in the world.

But when the public surged into our congregational life in September 2001, they chose to surge right back out after only a month or so. Of course, the nature of trauma recovery itself explains much of this behavior; once the initial shock passes so does some of the felt need for a spiritual sanctuary. But the psychological dynamics alone fail to account for why so few congregations said so little about the nation's pain,[18] and why so few visitors stayed for the long run. Perhaps they needed something more, some kind of spiritual power that transcends our compassion and our events; perhaps they needed to meet God and did not.

The Spirit dimension involves the infusion of God's presence and power into the venues (personal, electronic, institutional) in which the Church interacts with the sought. Sensitivity to this dimension comes from realizing that, no matter the depth of our relationship with the sought, only in a relationship with the Seeker are we "called out of darkness into wonderful light."[19] Just as some leaders reduce mission to membership, our perspective on the Spirit dimension risks reducing it either to a vague form of divine "background radiation," providing a comforting ambience for worship services, or to the extraordinary anointing carried by a heroic individual whose presence seems necessary for God's power to flow. Neither view serves the mission well. The former *de*personalizes the Holy Spirit into not much more than ambient energy for Christian events, and the latter *mis*personalizes the same Spirit as something like a battery used to power the ministry of big-personality leaders.

Peter rejected both perspectives when he refused Simon the Sorcerer's request to purchase his ability to fill believers with the Spirit. Acts 8 records the apostle's response to Simon as including these words: "You have no part or share in this ministry, because your heart is not right before God."[20] Simon saw the Spirit as a commodity up for sale and attempted to buy it as an enhancement to his career as a spiritual celebrity, the "Great Power" among the Samaritans. Peter's scathing response ("May your money perish with you!") makes a powerful statement about the dangers of confusing the Spirit with a benevolent force field, a renewable energy source, a handy talisman, or anything other than the Seeker empowering the Church and inviting the sought into a new life in Christ.

Where is God in our venues? Even some believers claim to experience little or no sense of God's presence in worship services. Keep in mind that Simon believed in Jesus and even experienced water baptism, but he still wanted to exchange money for access to the same Spirit who drew him to faith, putting the Holy Spirit on a par with the other deities he attempted to manipulate with his sorcery. Variations of this magical understanding of the Holy Spirit hinder mission by committing us unwittingly to the superstitious instead of the supernatural. The superstitious view conceives of the Spirit as either almost completely inaccessible (except by certain spiritual professionals) or almost completely controllable if the right spiritual exercises are performed.

But the Spirit of Christ operates in a realm transcending ours in which the Seeker is the sovereign, not the superstitious realm in which we or our representatives pretend to be sovereign. The Holy Spirit not only fills individuals to make the mission of Christ a reality; He reveals Christ to the sought on behalf of the Seeker. "We have not received the spirit of the world but the Spirit who is from God, that we may understand what God has freely given us," writes Paul, himself the product of a dramatic encounter with the Seeker on the road to Damascus. The Spirit forms the "mind of Christ" within us, filling our lives and relationships with power so that the sought can have the same mind in them.

Too often, the Church simply views mission in terms other than the power of God, perhaps because it is the one dimension of spatial evangelism over which we seem to have the least control. The early Church, possessing so little, demonstrated reliance on the Spirit that should challenge us today. The prayer meeting on behalf of the imprisoned apostles depicted in Acts 4 ends with this cry from the heart of the Church: " 'Now, Lord, consider their threats and enable your servants to speak your word with great boldness. Stretch out your hand to heal and perform miraculous signs and wonders through the name of your holy servant Jesus.' After they prayed, the place where they were meeting was shaken. And they were all filled with the Holy Spirit and spoke the word of God boldly."[21]

The same power operated in relationship with the sought when Paul met Lydia and her companions at a riverside Jewish prayer meeting near Philippi. Acts records that "the Lord opened her heart to respond to Paul's message."[22] Both the gospels and the book of Acts constitute a catalogue of supernatural encounters between the Seeker and the sought. Even Christ's followers who doubt that such events occur today admit that salvation itself requires a supernatural transaction of forgiveness and regeneration, and that the mission is resisted by powerful spiritual forces with which we cannot contend in our own strength.

Believers and environments filled with the Spirit create an atmosphere in which every stream of revelation can flow into the lives of the sought. The Spirit dimension is a product not of engineering but of a hunger and thirst for righteousness that God fills. This hunger is expressed in spiritual disciplines both on and off road, often an afterthought in the American Church, and also by the faith to take a chance on mission. It is no accident that many of the displays of God's power depicted in Scripture take place in a confrontation with evil or other desperate circumstance. A comfortable church that operates in safety, doing little more than tweaking existing structures, may never generate the level of dependence on God that is magnetic for the Spirit's power.

Common Wall Holiness

The three dimensions of the cube model represent only a simple illustration of the spatial principle. The value of this perspective stems from placing the dimensions into relationship with one another so that the size and shape of the Spirit's working area can be assessed. If mission fails to occur among us, some dimension of the cube impinges on the effect of the other dimensions. For example, a loveless people will eventually ruin even a perfect venue inhabited by the Spirit, and a compassionate faith community without ways of connecting with the sought celebrates God's presence without inviting others into the experience. In these and many other examples, shrinking any one dimension of the missional space possibly reduces the others almost to the vanishing point. This perspective offers not a neat geometric shape but the option of diagnosing weaknesses in mission by asking, "Is there any room for the mission here? If not, which dimension needs expanding?"

Answering this question honestly holds the potential for morphing the available space into a form that fits the context. A church I visited in Denmark, for instance, created a prayer and meditation chapel complete with candles and a fountain for use by the membership, but also to attract New Age people who related well to this environment. The chapel served as a connecting point for the sought, supplemented by large, public prayer services advertised only in New Age publications in which the pastoral staff prays for the specific needs of anyone who comes from the community, sometimes with dramatic results.

Paul described these many dimensions working together in his mission to the city of Thessalonica: "For we know, brothers loved by God, that he has chosen you, because our gospel came to you not simply with words, but also with power, with the Holy Spirit and with deep conviction. You know how we lived among you for your sake. You became imitators of us and of the Lord; in spite of severe suffering, you welcomed the message with the joy given by the Holy Spirit."[23]

Plainly, the heart dimension appears in the apostle's "deep conviction" and his reference to how he lived among them. The city itself, and specifically the synagogue there, formed the venue dimension for their relationship, with Paul and Silas taking the initiative in coming to the Thessalonians after their jailbreak in Philippi rather than demanding that they come to Jerusalem. The Spirit dimension appears as their message comes "with power, with the Holy Spirit" and results in the Thessalonians becoming "imitators" filled with the "joy given by the Holy Spirit." All three dimensions must function simultaneously for the missional life to grow into a reality and transform us in the process.

On a sidewalk in Dallas, I stand beside my friends Tony and Hannah outside a coffee house (called Insomnia) owned by their church at this time. Inside the small shop, bright, abstract artwork adorns the walls of the dark, narrow space where the patrons read, talk, and sip beverages so caffeinated they carry names like "The Lightning Bolt" and "The Electric Chair." While Christians operate the business here, I see no overt witness in any form and learn that even Christian bands who perform at Insomnia must limit their message to their music. The major attraction is the locally famous espresso milkshake and the neighborhood itself, with its national reputation as a home for alternative rock and roll and a club scene so vigorous that beer companies park semitrailers of product in alleyways to keep the bars stocked.

The impressive thing about Insomnia really happens once I am outside. The shop next door is called Condom Sense, the neighborhood sex store. I laugh with my friends about the way some Christians we know would react to the proximity of their ministry to a retail outlet specializing in sexual exotica. "Isn't the church going to be corrupted by a sex store?" they would ask, because they lack the love for the neighborhood that Tony and Hannah have in their hearts. "Couldn't you find some better location for the coffee house?" they would demand, able to envision only venues too safe for the sought to encounter people of the Spirit. "Aren't you afraid of being overwhelmed by temptation and just plain darkness?" they would complain, not finding the faith to believe that the Spirit who empowers us for mission can overcome any form of darkness.

I find the answers to all these questions by stepping back a few paces to get a photograph of how Insomnia and Condom Sense actually interface. I notice that the sex store has an armed security guard while the coffee house seems not to need one. The message is plain: you can pursue love in ways that require force to maintain order, or you can find love with a force that creates order, a broad way and a narrow way. The two stores are joined by a common block wall ten inches or so thick. If the one in us really is greater than the one in the world, ten inches is enough.

Chapter Eleven

Sacrifice

The Discipline of
Surrendering Preferences

The large hotel meeting room resembled many others: long, low-ceilinged, gloomy in the back and bright in the front. Between sessions I toured the display areas that rimmed the edges of the space, trying to understand the alien culture the organizers described as "generation X." As a newly appointed representative of my denomination, sporting the only suit and tie in the room and adorned with a lanyard-style "My Name Is Earl" tag, I walked up to two casually dressed young women sitting behind a vendor's exhibit table and asked my first-ever research question: "So, you're Xers, huh?" Both sets of twentysomething eyes hardened into a defensive expression that meant "shields up" and began shooting silent, anti-boomer rays to drive me off. It worked. I shrunk back into the gloom stung by the realization that my patronizing question treated these young people like exhibits, not exhibitors. From this experience, I conclude that a lot of good research begins badly.

But something else happened as well. This encounter represented the first time I ever suspected someone of refusing to speak to me because of my age and appearance. The whole exchange happened without the women behind the table saying a word. They did not need to. (Clearly, the dinosaur in the polyester suit before them was doomed to cultural obsolescence, so ignoring him was really the merciful thing to do. After all, why raise his hopes only to dash them later?)

My suspicion found confirmation in a conversation I overheard just a few hours later, involving the leader of the organization represented at the table I approached in the dark. One of his associates, referring to me, said, "Hey, did you know that guy over there is from the Assemblies of God?" implying that a connection might benefit us both. The leader of this nationally known young adult ministry replied tensely, "I know, I know," dismissing the associate's pleas and the opportunity without realizing that he had spoken loudly enough for me to hear. Once again, a younger leader found me unworthy of his time and attention. Though this interpretation may seem like middle-aged paranoia, similar experiences occurred too many times to signify only a misunderstanding. The most painful of them took the form of attending a young adult church in which no one spoke to us (except for the leadership and a few prior friends) for almost two years. Like some other groups I visit, the congregation's often-verbalized commitment to diversity and inclusiveness labored under an invisible age boundary: a gray ceiling.

This chapter outlines a partnership between the young and the old based on the spiritual discipline of sacrifice on issues of conscience. The mission of Jesus extends to all generations in all times and places, so it requires the kind of community in which "your young men will see visions, your old men will dream dreams."[1] The mission happens only if everyone involved is willing to make concessions. For the old, this often means releasing their grip on power and position (the subject of the next chapter) so that their hands are free to open doors for the follow-on generation. For the young, the mission requires living with less than the fullness of their preferences for the sake of synergy with their elders, in the certain knowledge that only God leads eternally; the rest of us have to let go eventually. The method by which Paul prepared Timothy for their travels together offers a case study in the off-road discipline of trading preferences for partnership.

Jews and Greeks

Timothy most likely came to faith in Christ, along with his mother and grandmother, during Paul's first visit to the city of Lystra (Acts 14), located in the region of Galatia. After circulating a letter from the leadership in Jerusalem dealing with the place of Gentiles in the Church, Paul returns to Lystra as part of his second missionary tour, one devoted to revisiting the churches founded during his first trip. He finds there, in Timothy, a young man of strong spiritual heritage and with such a good reputation that he is recognized as far away as Iconium (eighteen miles distant). This matter of reputation eventually becomes a criterion of eligibility for all Christian leaders.[2] Recognizing the potential in this young man, Paul decides to take him on the road to preach the good news about Jesus at every opportunity.

The apostle's selection of a protégé is doubly impressive given the unimpressive results achieved by John Mark, who had deserted Paul and Barnabas during their first missionary venture together. The issue of giving John Mark another chance grew so contentious that Paul and Barnabas split over it. Barnabas took John Mark with him to Cyprus, while Paul took Silas with him to Syria and Cilicia for the purpose of building up the churches. Ironically, this division over their first apprentice played a key role in sending Paul to Lystra short one protégé, perhaps preparing the way for Timothy. In the wake of John Mark's failure, many leaders would be tempted to avoid involving the inexperienced in ministry, but Paul, in biblical scholar William Barclay's words, "was always well aware of the necessity of training a new generation for the work that lay ahead."[3] His desire to model the mission simply outweighed any fear of failure, so "he wanted to take [Timothy] along on the journey."[4]

But Timothy posed a special challenge. Just prior to his visit to Lystra, Paul and others had begun representing the Council of Jerusalem to the Gentile churches, reassuring them that following Christ fully did not require observance of Jewish law and custom. This delicate mission and its carefully crafted official letter, reinforced by hand-picked messengers, met with a positive reception among the Gentiles. Paul and his band of traveling diplomats helped keep the peace between Jewish Christians in Jerusalem and Gentile believers in the Antioch region. But the solutions offered in the Council's policy letter (Gentile abstention from food sacrificed to idols, from blood, from the meat of strangled animals, and from sexual immorality) soon proved inadequate to address the life of just one man. As with many institutional solutions to divisive issues, temporary success on the organizational level immediately collided with seemingly irreconcilable predicaments on the personal level.

With a Jewish mother and a Greek father, Timothy's background created a paradox that abstaining from food offered to idols simply failed to resolve. In the ancient context, his family situation gave the father overall control of the home, but it put his religious upbringing in the hands of his mother. This heritage left Timothy in an awkward position. As New Testament scholar F. F. Bruce explains: "In the eyes of Jews, Timothy ranked as a Gentile because he had a Greek father and was uncircumcised. In the eyes of the Gentiles, however, he was practically a Jew, having been brought up in his mother's religion."[5]

In short, accompanying Paul created cultural problems for Timothy that generic provisions such as avoiding meat from strangled animals could not solve. Jewish opinion of the day differed over the legitimacy of children born in a mixed marriage. However, the failure to be circumcised, perhaps because his Greek father forbade it or because his mother held her Jewish convictions loosely at the time, doubtless served as an offense to some Jewish communities.

Paul addresses the dilemma of Timothy by circumcising him, "so he wouldn't offend the Jews who lived in those parts. They all knew that his father was Greek."[6] This decision contains two surprises: the first concerns the timing of the event, just after Paul stoutly resists attempts by hyperconservative Jewish Christians to impose circumcision on all Gentile converts; the other arises from the half-Greek Timothy's decision to go along with the idea. The first issue seems troubling because Paul appears to impose on Timothy exactly the rite from which he attempted to shield Gentile Christians in Antioch. Moreover, he served as one of the messengers announcing to the Gentiles that their new faith did not require becoming Jewish to become Christian. Yet now he requires that Timothy undergo this full initiation into Judaism before joining Paul on the road.

Circumcision predated the Law of Moses, finding its origin in God's relationship with Abram as a sign of God's covenant with him and a requirement for every male child eight days old.[7] The Mosaic Law codified an already permanent covenant ceremony making it a defining experience of male Jewish life both for those born within Israel and for proselytes joining the community from the outside. With notable gaps (such as the forty years of wilderness wandering), Israel maintained circumcision as an indicator of the covenant with God from the time of Abram until the day of Paul's arrival at Lystra in the middle of the first century A.D. Although the communities making up the Jewish Diaspora of the day held diverse views, circumcision maintained enormous currency and had serious implications for Christian mission. As the biblical commentator Stanley Horton notes, "Paul still went to the Jew first in every new city that he visited. For him to take an uncircumcised Jew into a synagogue would be like taking a traitor into an army camp."[8]

The circumcision of Timothy, then, represents a cultural, not theological, concession. Paul contends, for example, in his epistle to the church at Corinth that "circumcision is nothing and uncircumcision is nothing. Keeping God's commands is what counts."[9] He goes on to tell the Galatians that "the only thing that counts is faith expressing itself through love."[10] Given what we know of the Council of Jerusalem's decision depicted in Acts 15, Paul's perspective seems to represent what would become the majority position of the primitive Church. In Timothy's case, circumcision demonstrated Paul's full acceptance of Timothy as Jewish, removing any stigma associated with Timothy's mixed parentage and consequently avoiding a needless offense to Jewish hearers of the good news. In using a covenant sign to accomplish a cultural end, Paul used the very rite that could have been the most divisive to break down all national boundaries.

His credibility in making such a request of Timothy rests on Paul's personal practice of painful adaptation for the sake of the mission. As New Testament scholar Ajith Fernando concludes, "Paul not only insisted on costly discipleship for others, he modeled it in his own life."[11] Forgoing his rights as an apostle, he tells the Corinthians of his willingness to "put up with anything rather than hinder the gospel of Christ."[12]

Grace is free; mission is not. These sacrifices took two specific forms with regard to the grafting of the new Christian faith onto ancient Jewish tradition. First, Paul faced ongoing persecution and resistance from the most conservative sectors of the Jewish community over the sanctity of the Law in general. When the rumor spread among Jewish believers, for example, that he advocated a brazen (in their view) disregard for the Law of Moses, Paul took extra pains to demonstrate publicly his respect for the Law by engaging in ceremonial purifications and offerings at the temple in Jerusalem. Moreover, Acts 21 records that the mere suspicion that Paul brought a Greek (Trophimus the Ephesian) into the Temple area caused a riot requiring Roman military intervention to save Paul's life and quell the disturbance.

A second struggle centered on the question of mandatory circumcision of Gentile converts. "If I am still preaching circumcision, why am I still being persecuted?" he asks the Galatian church.[13] Though the issue seems resolved at the Council of Jerusalem, Paul faced it in concrete terms with regard to a second protégé, Titus, another son in the faith. He points out to his critics that even the apostolic leadership in Jerusalem did not require this Gentile disciple to undergo circumcision, refusing to concede to those who wanted to add the rite to faith and grace as prerequisites of salvation. Paul, who had been circumcised at eight days old, asks the half-Jewish, half-Greek Timothy to endure the same practice that he refuses to impose on the fully Greek Titus. The apparent contradiction resolves itself if we understand Paul's choice as signifying that salvation makes no ceremonial demands; otherwise "the offense of the cross has been abolished."[14] On the other hand, the mission that sent Jesus to the cross may involve painful personal concessions for us on behalf of others. The basic nature of Gentile Christianity defined by the leadership in Jerusalem did not require circumcision, but Paul exercises the freedom to ask for one of those voluntary concessions from his new protégé. When properly understood, grace elicits more sacrificial service than Law ever can.

Jewish Greeks

Timothy represents in some ways the younger leader of today who feels caught between two worlds, one dominated by the more traditional expressions of the Church (I'll call them the "Jews") and the other made up of the culture in which they are natives (the "Greeks"). As a product of both, these modern Timothys also attempt to navigate a morphing culture in which the only question seems to be the nature of the next change . Yet the "Jewish" world of traditional church that asks for their allegiance often seems so poorly suited for our highly fluid environment that they cringe at the thought of giving their lives to it. Many of these hybrid young people ask me privately, "Am I going crazy?" Or, after meeting a few peers experiencing the same stresses, they say with obvious relief, "I thought I was the only one!"

Another common reaction is their decision to plant new churches, a reaction based in part on unwillingness to work their way up in a system that often seems to them to have little future, or to endure the anguish of transitioning a traditional church into a contemporary or experimental form. They say things to me like, "I'm just not going to spend twenty years doing that." They cherish their "Jewish" heritage of conservative spiritual values but recognize that it now faces the challenge of the increasingly diverse, "Greek" world of which they are also citizens. The mingling of both influences makes our Timothys something like the children of cross-cultural missionaries: *third-culture people* who bond both to their homeland and to their adopted nation, creating a virtual citizenship that does not exactly represent either. We routinely meet natives of this culture among the young people who serve in our fellowship's missionary communities. Alexis, for example, appears on the surface to be an American Anglo in her twenties, but as the daughter of missionaries she is a Mexican in her soul. Faye, another

American about Alexis's age, looks the same but experiences the world as a person raised in Africa.

This new global citizenship carries the potential for personal confusion. Third-culture people often experience adjustment and identity struggles in their adopted nation and in their homeland, when they return. Their passport indicates U.S. citizenship, but their language, perspective, and personal style all say something else. The greatest challenge often occurs when they return to what is supposed to be their home country, only to feel out of sync in an unrecognizably alien land. This reverse culture shock carries a profound impact, sometimes moving people to return temporarily to their adopted country to blunt the feeling that they possess no real identity, no real home.

But every missional leader experiences shock, the only question being which kind. As a conservative Jewish leader, Paul commits to obeying his call to the Gentiles, which poses the supreme test, one for which he was prepared by a personal encounter with Christ on the road to Damascus. He displays both his heritage and his obedience by preaching in synagogues wherever available, but exercising the choice to turn to the Gentiles when necessary, reporting to his home base at Antioch that God had opened their hearts. Paul's challenge then involves identification with a group (the Gentiles) whom some of his conservative compatriots regard as people to be avoided, while others permit them to worship on the fringes of the synagogue. The Acts record seems to indicate that the closer to Jerusalem, the more difficult this identification, while Jewish acceptance of Gentile affiliation with their God becomes more common with distance—take, for example, Cornelius, the devout Roman centurion whose family lived at Caesarea.

Writing to his protégé years later, Paul explains that he embraced these Gentiles because "the grace of our Lord was poured out on me abundantly, along with the faith and love that are in Christ Jesus."[15] Grace and love still form the core of the identification between old and young. Joe, a campus missionary, served for many years among college students. One day over coffee, I asked him how he managed to stay relevant to them as his age advanced while theirs stayed frozen in the eighteen-to-twenty-two range. "Well," he replied, "I started out as their brother, I became their uncle, now I'm their father, and I guess there's only one stage left!" He found a way to identify with a subculture growing increasingly distant from his own experience because he loves students more than he loves his own preferences. Like a Hollywood leading man who extends his career by evolving into a character actor, wise older leaders treat identification with the young as a living thing that either grows or dies.

Timothy, on the other hand, faces the challenge of translating his Jewish-Greek background into an identity that fits with Jesus' mission. In one sense, his heritage overcomes the boundary between Jew and Gentile by combining them, but it simultaneously leaves him with the perplexing status of too-Greek-to-be-Jewish and too-Jewish-to-be-Greek. Does Timothy's hybrid life make him a Jew, a Gentile, both, or neither—and in whose eyes? One school of thought, represented by Bruce, suggests that Paul circumcised him because "it was better that [Timothy] be clearly one thing or the other than betwixt and between."[16] In this view, the young man's Jewish identity becomes primary as a result of submitting to this covenant sign, and his Gentile heritage fades into the background. The logic here revolves around Paul's strategy of going to the synagogues first whenever visiting a new city, a venue potentially closed to him if he brings along an apprentice viewed as a Gentile or an apostate Jew—both live options with Timothy in tow.

However, another interpretation, represented by theologian John Stott, argues the opposite: "His Jewish-Greek parentage would give him an entrée into both communities."[17] From this vantage point, Timothy's alloyed heritage serves not just as a passport into the Jewish community but as a natural connection to the much larger Gentile world. He embodies a perfect fit for Paul's calling to serve Jesus as an emissary to the Gentiles as well as to the nation of Israel. In the grace of God, Paul, the epitome of Jewishness, becomes the apostle to the Gentiles, joined by his half-Jewish, half-Greek disciple from Lystra. The older apostle reaches out for the new Gentile world of the Roman Empire from a Jewish perspective, while the younger man represents the transition to that new world in his mixed lineage.

But Timothy's ability to mold his life into a missional shape depends in part on his willingness to endure the pain of circumcision necessary to fit into a purpose larger than himself. Today, conforming one's life to the shape of something bigger than one's preferences is tantamount to sin in a society that rejects sacrifice and worships preference almost on the scale of idolatry. "Personal" computers connected to the Internet stand as altars to the religion of individual choice, which comes complete with "spiritual disciplines" (obsequious customer service, eBay shopping, mass customization). The goal is to avoid bending one's will to that of anything or anyone else. Growing up digital, younger people, who feel especially at home with this free agent ethos, face several identity challenges for a missional life.

The first of the challenges comes in the form of general attitudes toward sacrificial living. This issue became concrete for me during several conversations around the country with organizational leaders:

- *The airplane.* One conversation took place on an airplane as I sat beside the president of a nursing school. She complained about the difficulty of recruiting for her field. "Young people have so many opportunities and so much competition for their talents," she said, that convincing them to serve the public in a highly stressful profession such as nursing seemed to grow more difficult by the day—unless the candidates were identified young. I asked how young; her answer: "The fifth grade." Later than that, and too many good options make nursing noncompetitive.
- *The church.* In Texas I asked a church's media producer how he recruits the staff it takes to organize and produce their high-tech services. He smiled and told me they bring young people in at the age of twelve. A glance into the room next door, where a junior

high school student was focused on a Mac as if his life depended on it, confirmed the producer's account. Not only do twelve-year-olds simply enjoy better computer skills than older people (say, twenty-year-olds); they also have the time to invest in the ministry. Just a few years later, their schedule will be filled with other activities, squeezing out even media ministry.

This pair of simple examples highlight some of the attitudinal and practical barriers to divesting myself of "my rights" (that is, the right to remain uncircumcised, to forgo sacrifice) and investing myself in something outside my personal preferences. As I revise this chapter, I talk with a midlife missionary over the Internet about his personal struggle with "stepping back" from the ministry frontline to assume vital strategic and managerial roles that are behind the scenes. Other, younger people now inherit the role he once relished. Having done the same, I feel his pain. The challenge is not just for the young.

Tension abounds over how our Timothys, our younger leaders, will or will not fit into the existing Church in its local and denominational expressions. As third-culture natives, how do they find a home in a Church that remains largely "Jewish," at least in their eyes? One young leader who I'll call Andrew pleaded with his older peers in an e-mail: "We love you guys, we want to be a part of this . . . give us the leeway to figure some things out." He went on to note the cultural disconnect between his denomination's "Jewish" events and the "Greeks" he serves:

> After leaving the bookstore, I went into the service where, between a dynamic time of worship and the anointed speaker . . . the presence of the Lord was beaten to death with a shovel as [an official] hijacked the meeting to take a brief 45 minutes to drone on and on about a bunch of stuff that will just make your ears bleed. But that's another rant altogether—forgive me.
>
> Here's the postmodern part. Now, this lady is sweet, but she is like 1,000 years old—not that there's anything wrong with that—

and she tries—God bless her she tries. So in the middle of this speech that Fidel Castro would think was too long, she says, "And we want to reach out to the postmodern women too." So now I woke up, right, and then she says, "I want all of you ladies in here who are under 35 to stand up . . . we love you postmodern women." What? That's all it takes to be postmodern now—a birth certificate issued after 1968? *Who taught these people this word?* And how can we make them stop using it?

In a later interview, I asked Andrew to speculate on the reaction of the very Greek people in his church to the sort of regional minister's convention he describes. His response: "They would freak out, what have you brought us to, you've tricked us, this is some kind of cult . . . culturally it is so, so different." His very progressive church simply would not prepare his members (many of whom have only recently found faith) for such a traditional event. In fact, Andrew takes pains to insulate his members from their own denomination to avoid just such a collision! Yet his affinity with the core beliefs of his fellowship remains strong: "The substance, I'm more convinced of than any time in my life. . . . I'm not going to go naked, but I'm also not going to wear the clothes of the 1970s."

Andrew represents a sizeable under-thirty-five leadership subculture that I encountered during a three-year interview project. I suspect he speaks for many, many others across all Christian fellowships.[18] Cameron Strang, for example, the founder of Relevant Media, argues that "my generation is discontented with dead religion." Speaking of his shaved head, beard, and earrings, he continues: "If we looked like goody-two-shoes, clean cut, we couldn't have a conversation with our lesbian friend at the coffee shop, because she couldn't relate." Generalizing to the post-Christian population, Lee Rabe, pastor of Threads, an alternative church in Kalamazoo, Michigan, says: "The deity-free 'church lite' of the megachurches, that's the last thing these people want. . . . They want to talk about God. It's hard-core, not in a fire and brimstone way, but it has to be raw, real."[19] As with most of the young leaders I meet, these statements arise not from a radical theology but from a radical discomfort with the culture of the "Jerusalem church."

Older or conservative leaders, strongly identified with this Jerusalem church ministry culture, respond too frequently with a dismissive or disciplinary attitude toward their "Greek" brothers and sisters, sometimes framing them as outright rebels and at other times simply ignoring them. Dialogue quickly disintegrates into diatribe, in which both sides ironically take the same position: "My form of intolerance is the only form we're going to tolerate around here." The currency of this issue asserted itself in a meeting with around fifty young church leaders in the Pacific Northwest. Given the opportunity to choose any agenda for our time together, their suggestions all revolved around just one problem: how are younger and older leaders going to get along? Launching the discussion, I stepped back and watched them pass the wireless microphone among themselves, contributing their concerns, their pain, and their wisdom. I noted the almost total lack of any need for stimulation from me as the intensity of the discussion drove them forward. How are what we called *Smallville* leaders and *Law and Order* leaders going to coexist? "How can we make the table bigger," one of them asked, "including *Smallville* without kicking *Law and Order* out?"

I Choose the Mission

The early Church faced the same issues. How could a Jewish Gentile like Timothy fit into Paul's life and mission? Their relationship suggests the criteria for defining a way to work together.

Voluntary

Timothy consented to being circumcised. Paul did not intimidate or overpower him, or even talk him into it. Timothy recognized that without this sign of God's covenant with the Jewish people, some members of his own nation would simply be unable to receive him and his message. Using force to achieve cultural homogeneity always achieves the opposite, imposing a penalty rather than eliciting a sacrifice. The notion of mandatory circumcision for Timothy (or, comparably, mandatory allegiance to a particular church culture for younger leaders today) creates only a temporary and superficial conformity without a circumcision of the heart. To call out the best in these leaders, sacrifice must be a choice, not a mandate.

Sacrificial

The physical rigors of this procedure in Timothy's life hardly require elaboration, but the spiritual significance speaks loudly too. Paul's disciple simply chose to forgo his personal preference for comfort to become part of something that transcended both him and Paul. Though none of us faces a similar physical challenge, all of us (especially the young) deal with the issue of whether the sacrifices required to affiliate with the larger Church (a denomination, network, or congregation) are worth it. Biblical scholar Ajith Fernando suggests one way to answer this question:

> Others might avoid the pain of submitting themselves to circumcision, but for Timothy to succeed in ministry he had to take this on. This was the pain of identification with people. One who loves to eat meat may need to become a vegetarian if he finds that eating meat will be a stumbling block to the Buddhists he is trying to reach. . . . One who is trying to reach people in the slums may need to live near the place where the people she wants to reach live. As a result, she may have to endure the pain and terror of having her house broken into. . . . Most people will avoid such things, but we should voluntarily take these things on in order to bear fruit that really lasts.[20]

Frequently, in conversation with frustrated young leaders I lean on the metaphor of family—your organization is your family, and we all know that the word is (sometimes) a synonym for *dysfunction*.

The question becomes, then, how to know which forms of pain to embrace as genuinely necessary to be part of a family and involved in God's mission, and which ones to regard as contrived and imposed. I think the answer lies in the nature of the goal—being missional.

Timothy's willingness to tolerate circumcision, like Paul's willingness to endure beatings and shipwrecks, stemmed from his love for God and his mission of redemption among the sought. As Stott puts it, "What was unnecessary for acceptance with God was advisable for acceptance among some people."[21]

Missional

Those people awaited in Europe, where Timothy would join Paul in preaching the gospel in response to a night vision in which Paul heard a man say, "Come over to Macedonia and help us."[22] Their travels together brought them into contact with Jewish synagogues across the Roman Empire, validating Timothy's sacrificial choice. Some conservative commentators even regard him as possibly the first Gentile convert to become a missionary himself.

Painful adjustments receive their validity from the degree to which they voluntarily enhance our ability to live the mission of Jesus together. This sort of partnership between the old and the young requires the old to surrender power and the young to lay down preferences, an especially difficult challenge for third-culture leaders to whom the "vibe" means so much. Hundreds of hours of interviewing have convinced me that the majority of doctrinal disputes in our fellowships represent only symptoms of underlying cultural divisions. Distinctive teachings are a lightning rod for the energy of discontent. Bringing the sides together means raising the profile of mission (not just missions) so that distinctives no longer represent the highest point in the organization, the one attracting all the energy. I have seldom met a young leader who wouldn't stick around if this emphasis on mission prevailed enough to achieve practical outcomes such as tolerance for a diversity of ministry styles, canceling the veto power that existing churches have over new plants in their communities, leadership that resources the vision of the churches rather than attempting to define that vision, and so forth.

For the young, this renewal of mission means that someone sacrifices—perhaps even their right to leave. One young leader sorely tested in his relationship with his denomination e-mailed this example: "I have committed to stick with [my denomination] though, and I will follow through with that. I start my pre-med degree next semester to prepare to do medical mission work in the future." Mission is a powerful adhesive, motivating us to sacrifice our preferences in a way that nothing else can. When we demote mission by prioritizing a certain brand of Christian culture, sacrifice dies because no proprietary interpretation of what the Church should look like is worth the pain. As Andrew put it, "I'm called to reach people who don't know this stuff . . . like the guys in my church who ask me, 'now, what's the resurrection?'. . . If I had to choose between those people and [the fine points of] a doctrinal statement, that's not a hard decision to make."

The critical task for organizational leaders involves realizing that their constituents who are sympathetic to a third-culture perspective will indeed opt out if defending the group's identity seems more important than the reason the group exists. One young leader after another has expressed this to me in interviews. Even an older colleague with a lifetime of service to his fellowship told me with tears, "If the choice is between the mission and the organization . . . I choose the mission." Who could condemn those who decide that their relationship with a certain organization has become the necessary sacrifice if the mission is at stake? But when the purposes of God captivate our hearts, leaders of all kinds willingly endure cultural hardship for the sake of the whole. Perhaps at one time mission depended on organization. Today, organization depends on mission. Younger leaders need to ask themselves what they will sacrifice for the sake of concerted effort. Older leaders need to ask themselves whether what they represent is worth sacrificing for.

Chapter Twelve

Legacy

The Discipline of Passing the Baton

I received an almost fatal shock one beautiful Sunday afternoon, as a server at a hotel restaurant cleared away the dishes from a nice after-church lunch with our friends Randy and Heidi and their children. Just after the check arrived, sitting across the table from me, Randy began to laugh while calculating the tip and fishing for his credit card. When I asked what he found so humorous, he produced the bill: it announced my very first senior citizen's discount in a restaurant—unsolicited. The discount cost me much more in chagrin than the two dollars it saved my hosts.

The best refuge when this reality places its cold hand on one's shoulder takes the form of thinking about seventy-eight million peers facing the same crisis. The front edge of the baby boomer generation is reaching retirement age, with one boomer turning sixty every 7.7 seconds as of New Year's Day 2006. Even those of us still on the near side of this divide can see it from here, with AARP reminding us of our destiny about every other month when yet another membership card arrives. I immediately throw it into the trash—just before I take my Lipitor. The self-assured mantras of my generation included "Don't trust anyone over thirty!" "Power to the people!" "O Lord, won't you buy me a Mercedes Benz?" and "It's only rock and roll, but I like it." Those are the slogans of a generation who believed they would shake off the shackles of history to change the world.

Then life happened. If today we re-composed some of the best known of our popular music hits, the titles might sound something like this:

- Herman's Hermits: "Mrs. Brown, You've Got a Lovely Walker"
- Bobby Darin: "Splish, Splash, I Was Havin' a Flash"
- Ringo Starr: "I Get By with a Little Help from Depends"
- Roberta Flack: "The First Time Ever I Forgot Your Face"
- Paul Simon: "Fifty Ways to Lose Your Liver"[1]

The humor in this sort of sarcasm stems from the undeniable truth facing a cohort that believes, with our peer Rod Stewart, that we will be "forever young." In my mind, the basket remains one step from the foul line, my waist never gets larger than thirty-four inches, and my hair still occupies the top of my head. My brain feels eighteen years old—still listening to the Stones on what was called a transistor radio—only my body lets me down. For my male tribe, then, the life of rock and roll, adrenalin, and testosterone somehow became a life of John Tesh, Prozac, and Viagra. The severity of the shock we feel in response to this change reveals our commitment to a permanent position as youthful arbiters of culture. We never counted on living the backside of the curve.

We boomers set out to change the world, but it changed us too, especially in the form of the three Ms: Marriage, Mortgage, and Midlife. In fact, a recent study by the Pew Foundation finds that the generation who planned on revolutionizing society, now in its late middle years, tends to live decidedly conventional lives.[2] We buy homes in cities such as Dallas and Akron, work for companies such as Allstate and Century 21, sell our old Led Zeppelin albums on eBay, and scheme to get even larger television screens. Our divorce rate stands 500 percent higher than that of our parents, who we thought knew nothing. Listening to NPR in our SUVs, we cling to the illusion of youth with hair implants, vitamin elixirs, Botox injections, and late-night infomercial exercise machines. But we hold on. After all, if the Rolling Stones can still tour, maybe there is hope for us.

Lunch, so to speak, is over, and the check has arrived. Boomers now lead 60 percent of America's churches. Bill Easum summarizes the research on the state of the Church during our watch: "In another 50 years Christianity will have about the same influence in the U.S. as it does in Canada or Europe."[3] Walking the streets of northern Europe, passing one darkened house of worship after another, touring cities in which the odds of meeting a Christ follower hover around one in a hundred, I find Easum's prediction taking on a frightening reality. Even if his forecast misrepresents the future by a fairly wide margin (which I do not believe), my tribe needs to think seriously about building a bridge to the next generation of leaders, about how to pass the baton to younger people who can create a church truly indigenous to our times. Many of these leaders doubtless intend simply to go it alone, but this chapter makes a case for the off-road discipline of baton passing, which will be required if we are to develop a cooperative relationship between the generations and set the stage for transition rather than amputation or exodus.

God's Retirement Plan

The apostle Paul wrote to his younger protégé, Timothy, in a way that speaks to this contemporary challenge of baton passing. Visiting the city of Lystra around A.D. 47, Paul found Timothy in the crowd, the son of a Jewish-Christian mother and a Greek father, as we discussed in the last chapter.[4] Hearing good things about this new Christ follower, he brought Timothy into his traveling missionary band and set off to preach Jesus in the provinces of the Roman Empire. Years later, Timothy led the church in the city of Ephesus, a prominent economic and spiritual center in the Roman province of Asia Minor.

In many important ways, Timothy inherited this ministry from Paul.[5] The younger man served as an extension of Paul's work in Macedonia; accompanied him in his travels; and served as his emissary to Corinth, Philippi, and Thessalonica (Paul described him to the Corinthians as "carrying on the work of the Lord just as I am"). Timothy preached Christ in Corinth; was mentioned in the introduction to six of Paul's epistles, often as "our brother"; was described to the Romans as "my fellow worker"; and was imprisoned and released for the gospel's sake.

Paul and Timothy represent an exemplar of passing the baton from one generation of leadership to another. The first few verses of 2 Timothy, along with other New Testament passages, define the traits of a successful baton handoff in the relationship between these two runners. When Paul writes, near the end of his life, "I have fought the good fight, I have finished the race, I have kept the faith,"[6] his words to Timothy convey a sense of contentment in the face of imminent execution, encouraging Timothy to "do your best to come to me quickly."[7] Using Paul's relay race metaphor, his legacy takes the form of a handoff of the baton to Timothy, among others, ensuring that the fledgling churches he founded would not perish in his absence. Despite many problems and issues, Timothy leads a church founded by Paul, running his lap successfully with the leadership baton in his hand. I believe that baton passing represents God's retirement plan for older leaders, and that cooperating with this plan requires several traits.

Love

Paul's personal affection for his protégé finds expression in the opening verses of his second letter: "Timothy, my dear (in Greek, beloved) son: Grace, mercy and peace from God the Father and Christ Jesus our Lord."[8] In his first letter, Paul refers to Timothy as "my true (in Greek, genuine, true-born) son in the faith."[9] In 1 Corinthians 4:17, he adds, "my son, who I love, who is faithful to the Lord." Clearly, love forms the bond between the two runners, stimulating Paul to hand off in order to receive the pure joy of watching Timothy run toward his own finish line.

Passing the baton begins in the heart with loving the handing off more than the holding on. This transaction poses a real challenge for older leaders who still think of themselves as forever young. George Barna, a member of the boomer tribe, offers an explanation and a confession in this regard: "The sticking point is our core value:

power. We love power. We live for power. Power lunches, power ties, power suits, power offices, power titles, power cars, power networks. . . . Boomers revel in power. The sad result is that most Boomers—even those in the pastorate or in voluntary, lay-leadership positions in churches—have no intention of lovingly handing the baton to Baby Busters."[10]

The most painful evidence of this reality shows up in congregations (sometimes very large ones) experiencing a form of conflict potentially much more dangerous than the so-called worship wars of the 1990s. Struggles over leadership succession around the country, in which the baton serves as a weapon, would make a corporate raider blush. The root of these destructive conflicts is often older leadership that is unwilling to let go, and unable to face the reality that their tenure is at an end, which costs them the opportunity to prepare a succeeding generation.

A middle-aged couple approached me in the aisle after a conference presentation wearing earnest expressions and bringing a serious question: "If the way you describe young adults is accurate, we're concerned about whether we can leave the church to these people!" During moments like this, I thank God that, in His wisdom, He created us with a voluntary circuit breaker between our thoughts and our words. In my mind, I shouted back, "Who do you think you are to write off a whole generation as unfit for duty? I know one of your kids, and I would be proud to have her as the pastor of my church!" But out of my mouth came just six quiet words: "Well, . . . no one else is coming."

The issue of motivation, then, centers not on racing technique or choosing the right equipment but on whether letting the baton go represents a joy or a threat to me—whether I can, with Paul, rejoice in the success of a younger person, even as the end of my own run approaches. Older leaders routinely give lip service to the necessity of developing the younger generation. But when I hear these speeches, I get the sense that we elders often operate from a mental picture that envisions the new cohort as strikingly similar to ourselves—in other words, a junior version of us. Similarly, letter writers of Paul's day routinely claimed to be thinking constantly of their readers, giving lip service to a social convention, but Paul brings something special to his epistle: "Night and day I constantly remember you in my prayers. Recalling your tears, I long to see you, so that I may be filled with joy."[11] Instead of just talking to Timothy about God, he talks to God about Timothy, remembering the tears he shed when they last parted, perhaps at Paul's second arrest by the Romans. For Paul, time together with his protégé meant being filled with joy. If we have no tears for the young and no joy with them, what possible value will they find in our words? Older leaders need to ask themselves, "For whom do I weep?"

The motivation to hand off comes from simple personal affection born out of relationship. These two men walked the roads of the Roman Empire together, facing danger and hardship, announcing the good news about Jesus in the power of God, sleeping outside, sometimes eating and sometimes not, sometimes treated like kings and sometimes like criminals. They bonded by the sort of experience that formed in Paul a paternal feeling. "Timothy has proved himself," he writes to the Philippians, "because as a son with his father he has served with me in the work of the gospel. . . . I have no one else like him, who takes a genuine interest in your welfare."[12] Most pointedly, in the introduction of this letter to Philippi the elder apostle describes both himself and his younger friend as simply "servants of Christ."[13] The knowledge of the one whom they serve levels all other differences of age and culture between them.

Paul gladly releases the baton because the next lap belongs not to a staffer, or a functionary, or a drone, or an enemy, but to a son, a man whom he both loved and liked in a way that develops only out of investing time. Paul hints at the difficulty of implementing this simple principle when he writes to the Corinthians: "Even though you have ten thousand guardians in Christ, you do not have many fathers, for in Christ Jesus I became your father through the gospel."[14] Many of the young leaders I meet know the sting of orphan status, deprived by their elders of both fatherly affection and professional example. Speaking for many twentysomethings, Ron sent me these comments by e-mail:

> I have felt so beaten down and exhausted for years because I feel almost as if I've been having to fight to be myself in the fellowship, and I have been a victim of the abuses of the church and have experienced many people who are not willing to pass the baton to my generation. . . . I know many people my age (20s) who have considered many times leaving the fellowship (though they desperately want to stay) because of the refusal to pass the baton to the next generation. I myself have considered leaving the fellowship for the same reason.

This generation needs fathers and mothers in the faith, who love to hand off more than to hold on because they are able to enjoy success coming to someone other than themselves and because they love mission more than they love power. My friends Randy and Mark represent one of the best relay teams I have ever seen. While planting a church in the Cleveland area, Randy, a card-carrying boomer, developed a relationship of mutual respect with Mark, a gen X associate pastor. Several years later, when Randy felt a call to take a leave of absence to do missionary work with a parachurch agency, he handed off leadership of the congregation to Mark and moved out of town for two years. Randy's return was always meant to be a negotiated experience, in which neither he nor Mark knew if the arrangement would be permanent. But their trust in one another (and their credibility in the eyes of the church) made the relationship work. The church has expanded to a second site under Mark's leadership, and Randy's thriving missionary work has indeed become a permanent assignment.

Integrity

In addition to love, those holding the baton must own something worth passing along. "I have been reminded of your sincere faith," Paul reminisces about Timothy.[15] The term *reminded* here implies that something external has happened to jog Paul's memory. Perhaps some other faithful young man spoke or behaved in a way that made Paul think, "Why, that's just like Timothy!" meaning that his apprentice was never far from this thoughts. Paul goes on to identify the source of Timothy's faith: it "first lived in your grandmother Lois and in your mother Eunice and, I am persuaded, now lives in you also."[16] The legacy of these believing generations took concrete form in his life: "From infancy you have known the holy Scriptures, which are able to make you wise for salvation through faith in Christ Jesus."[17] Timothy received a legacy of personal devotion to God's word from his believing family, a powerful example of the potential of baton passing among generations.

That day in Lystra, Paul fused his life to Timothy's heritage by inviting him into his mission as "an apostle of Christ Jesus by the will of God, according to the promise of life that is in Christ Jesus."[18] In other words, Paul owns something, a life and a mission, worth inheriting. Fretting over the merits of those who receive the baton distracts us from asking if our lives offer anything worth passing on. If we are living (as one youth pastor put it to me recently) "a gospel that doesn't work," why would anyone want our baton? The question of who inherits our legacy must be secondary to the issue of whether we leave anything by way of example and relationship that qualifies as valuable. Lois and Eunice got it right; their own walk with God drew Timothy to imitate them. They understood a basic dynamic of legacy: we are not what we have; we are what we leave. My friend Scott, for example, who pastors a large church near Dallas, knows the joy of succeeding his own father, Tom, who remains on the staff leading the classic Sunday morning service while Scott preaches in the contemporary service. Tom (who is completing a doctoral degree and coordinates the congregation's growing network of schools) relates to his Sunday morning audience with an accordion. Scott uses video clips. But both father and son are part of the same relay team, one that will win the race.

Faith

Baton passers have to place as much faith in the next runner as they place in themselves. The fastest runner on a relay team is always positioned in the anchor lap, the final sprint to the finish line. Paul speaks to the source of that runner's speed when he reminds Timothy "to fan into flame the gift of God, which is in you through the laying on of my hands. For God did not give us a spirit of timidity, but a spirit of power, of love and of self-discipline."[19] His potential speed arises out of much more than just his natural talent. Paul noted this distinction in his first letter: "I give you this instruction in keeping with the prophecies once made about you, so that by following them you may fight the good fight."[20] His mentor reminds Timothy that the prophetic promise at the heart of his ministry reaches its potential only to the extent that the "gift of God" operates within him. Gen. William Booth, founder of the Salvation Army, once wrote, "The tendency of fire is to go out; watch the fire on the altar of your heart." When the gift ignites, Paul admonishes, timidity about life and mission gives way to "a spirit of power, of love and of self-discipline."[21]

The potential of the follow-on generation defines itself by the operation of the Holy Spirit in their hearts and lives, not by congruence with their elders on issues such as appearance and perspective. Imagine the reaction if all of the ministers in my fellowship, the Assemblies of God, received an e-mail announcing that a twenty-six-year-old has just been named as an executive leader on the national level. "Nonsense!" some might cry. "We can't have some kid guiding a fellowship with millions of adherents!" others might complain. Congratulations: this attitude disqualifies J. Roswell Flower, the first Secretary-Treasurer of the Assemblies of God.[22] No wonder Paul admonished Timothy not to let anyone "look down on you because you are young."[23] At midlife and beyond, forgetting the considerable accomplishments of young people becomes easier and easier. In my fellowship's first generation, for example, some of our churches were planted and pastored by men and women not much older than teenagers, a practice found only in history books today.

God can use the natural speed of the runner who receives the baton. We trust ultimately in the work of the Spirit of God in a heart completely yielded to the mission of Jesus to seek and save the lost. I witness this fanning of the flame regularly among younger friends: Anthony, planting a nontraditional church among post-Christians in Austin; Tim, working as a bivocational missionary to the Internet; Randy, growing a young adult ministry in Arkansas; Bethany, working tour after tour on the Mercy Ships; and the youngest missionaries who seem willing to go to the hardest places. The task of the older leader is not to judge Timothy or conform him, but remind him of the workings of the Spirit in his life and encourage him to fan the gift into flame. After drinking an ocean of coffee with leaders like this around the country, I have learned more than how to load songs into an iPod or set up an RSS feed on my Web browser. A generation waits in their lane for the baton, intending to "run with perseverance the race marked out for us."[24]

The value of a connection to older leaders involves much more than simply filling slots emptied by those of us who will migrate into AARP. The elder runner models how to relinquish power to the younger, for whom life guarantees the same challenge one day. In twenty more years, for example, today's twenty-year-olds face a conversation with people half their age that might go something like this: "Didn't you guys used to have a thing called, let's see, was it the multinet? No, the Internet! That was before computers were implanted in our earlobes. And those T-shirts and jeans you wore to church; wow! I saw some on the 'Antiques Road Show' holocast— you know, the one that's beamed to your sunglasses. What a hoot! Everyone knows that tuxedos are the only thing to wear to church." A day of handing off beckons even the youngest and the hippest. Until that day arrives, older leaders hold an obligation to illustrate with their own lives how people who love mission more than power give up the latter for the sake of the former.

No One Else Is Coming

Paul cannot help Timothy understand the mission by sitting in the stands shouting, "Run faster! Run faster!" Rather, as one who is about to finish his own race, he issues an invitation from prison to his son in the faith, one runner to another, with these words: "So do not be ashamed to testify about our Lord, or ashamed of me his prisoner. But join with me in suffering for the gospel, by the power of God."[25] Join with me. Those receiving the baton will commit fully to the race if they see older people doing the same, with the goal of forming a partnership that expands everyone's potential. The condition of the American Church certainly suggests the opportunity—in fact, the necessity—of collaboration among missional people.

Younger runners snatch the baton and dash for the finish line in response to the love and trust of the elders they respect for running a good race. The older invite the younger to join the relay by the offer of the baton, involving them in important aspects of mission right now. Both sides of the relationship are invited by God to "press on toward the goal to win the prize for which God has called me heavenward in Christ Jesus."[26] Only mutual dependence on each other and shared devotion to the mission of Jesus create the conditions for winning this race. If either side hesitates, the baton is dropped, raising the specter of an anchor lap run by leaders who lack the kick to finish and aren't self-aware enough to know they don't have it.

While talking to a class recently on the state of the Church in America, I saw one of our students use the seminary's wireless Internet to e-mail his son about the issue under discussion that day. (I encourage every class participant to be online at all times.) He asked Tyler, a student at a Christian university, what he felt the Church would need to look like in the twenty-first century. This is his slightly edited reply:

> Honestly, I don't believe that one particular way will work. . . . it takes
> a mix of coffeehouse/deep thinking opportunities, pizza/no thinking
> opportunities, gift giving/unexpected opportunities, God experiences,

music music music, and decent tv shows. . . . we have to go to where they are and not intrude but inspire creative (and uplifting) thought. . . .

there's enough teaching of damnation, I think it's time to just love. . . .

that's the only thing that will work

America doesn't need God. . . . She doesn't realize that her heart is slowly being burst through depression, personal confusion, gluttony, selfishness, and brainless acts of "freedom" . . . the church can't be church anymore. . . .

yeah it will reach the [church kids], but not the rejects. . . .

Single parent homes, substance abuse, unrestrained sexual activity . . . "failure" looms over every teenage head. . . . what can we do other than communicate purpose. . . .

Employers, teachers, musicians, and the philosophically-apt, will have a big part in the next revival. . . .

I see the church as taking a whole different form . . . the underground. . . .

you mentioned overseas. . . . we've got to treat Christianity as if we're in a place that needs it . . . because we are, but no one seems to know that.

I could pass out all the tracts and put up millions of posters, but ultimately, those people aren't in my circle of influence. . . .

the church is going to take on a whole different definition of "embracing" the world . . . or we will miss what we're here for. . . .

those are my random thoughts for now. . . . talk to me about what you're thinking. . . this is fun!

Adios,

your son Tyler

The Tylers of today must lead the American Church just months from now. For that to happen tomorrow, Tyler must become someone's son in the faith today. An older leader must pray for him, love him, and involve him right now, passing the baton to him and his generation. No one else is coming.

Epilogue:
Three Coffee Houses

This book is really the story of three coffee shops in Springfield, Missouri. The Mud House is where it all started—not the writing, but the realization that off-road disciplines change everything. With that concept in hand, much of the draft writing happened at Cassil's Coffee, where my friend Kevin provided the supportive atmosphere (and free wireless) that made the words come more easily. A franchise place called Panera Bread was the scene of most of the final editing, a location chosen because of the lowest probability of interruption (given that I know few people who go there). Three coffee houses, three stages taking me from connectivity to isolation.

What's interesting to me is that my seminary office never became a productive venue for writing this book—too many Christians there, and too many Christian things to occupy my attention. There is life among God's people, but there is also life among the sought. I remember the days when people went into their offices to work alone and emerged for meetings to work collaboratively. But I leave my door open all the time, so for me the office is where I see people most (the core of our team's collaboration), and I go off site for quiet and for the kind of contact with the sought that is the oxygen of this project.

A lot has happened since I started writing. I have traveled more than ever, blogged (www.xanga.com as Coffeedrinkinfool), moved to another house, experimented with manuscript preaching, bought surfer sandals in San Diego, started a Website (www.earlcreps.com), provided spiritual direction for some Christian organizations, preached in settings ranging from traditional Anglo to African-American to posteverything, sipped coffee made by a machine in Denmark, and started working out on an elliptical exerciser. Along the way, I have met a whole new set of friends. Perhaps their stories will write the next book.

But I am worried. Having started out at the edgy Mud House, a favorite of local Indy rockers, I gravitated to Kevin's delightful suburban coffee house and restaurant (because it was closer to my new house) and today am writing these words in the Panera Bread franchise. (I flirted with Starbucks, but it didn't last.) Over the course of writing, I fear this migration represents something larger, a gradual drifting from the root of the experience (up close connection with the sought at the Mud House and Cassil's) to a more orderly, franchise-style distance that achieves the isolation I need for working, but at the penalty of having many fewer spiritual conversations. In other words, even though the book has become the vehicle for what I truly believe about the off-road disciplines, the process of writing it may have pushed me back on road in some ways. I cannot live with that trade-off.

The only answer, I think, is to make staying off road itself a sort of *meta-discipline*, arranging my life so God gets a chance to take the initiative. This means spending time in places and with people where God is very active—in other words, among the sought whom God loves so much. So, I'm outa here. It's back to the Mud House downtown and Kevin's in the 'burbs, each the home to a different sort of sought person. Get the French press ready, friends. I'm back.

Notes

Introduction

1. Bosch, D. *Transforming Mission: Paradigm Shifts in Theology of Mission*. Maryknoll, N.Y.: Orbis, 1991, p. 300.
2. Inskeep, K. W., and Drake, J. L. "Worship Attendance in the Evangelical Lutheran Church of America: Faith Communities Today." n.d. [http://www.elca.org/RE/reports/ccspwrsp1.PDF]; Woods, J. "New Tasks for Congregations: Reflections on Congregational Studies." n.d. [http://www.resourcingchristianity.org/downloads/essays/J%20Woods%20Essay.pdf]; Barna, G. *Rechurching the Unchurched*. Venture, Calif.: Isaachar Resources, 2000, p. 129.
3. Foster, R. *Celebration of Discipline: The Path to Spiritual Growth*. New York: HarperCollins, 1978.
4. Foster (1978), p. 1.
5. John 3:30.
6. John 20:21.

Chapter One

1. 1 Timothy 4:15.
2. Galatians 2:20.
3. 3 Philippians 3:20.
4. Galatians 6:14.
5. John 17:14.

6. Ellis, J. "All the News That's Fit to Blog." *Fast Company*, Apr. 2002 [http://www.fastcompany.com/online/57/jellis.html].
7. John 20:21.
8. Acts 19:1–7.
9. 1 Peter 5:3.

Chapter Two

1. "Number of Unchurched Adults Has Nearly Doubled." *Barna Update*, May 4, 2004 [http://www.barna.org/FlexPage.aspx?Page =BarnaUpdate&BarnaUpdateID=163].
2. Olson, D. "The State of the Nation." *PowerPoint* [http://www. theamericanchurch.org/]. See also Smietana, B. "Statistical Illusion." *Christianity Today*, Apr. 2006 [http://www.christianitytoday. com/ct/2006/004/32.85.html].
3. Matthew 16:18.
4. 1 Corinthians 13:12.
5. Romans 8:35.
6. Heath, C. "How to Get Bad News to the Top." *Fast Company*, Sept. 2002 [http://www.fastcompany.com/online/62/badnews. html].
7. Hill, D. "Reaching the Post-Christian." *Leadership Journal* [http://ctlibrary.com/12099].
8. U.S. Congregational Life Survey, 2002 [http://www.uscongregations. org/]; "Asians and the Affluent Are Increasingly Likely to Be Born Again," *Barna Update*, May 30, 2000 [http://www.barna. org/FlexPage.aspx?Page=BarnaUpdate&BarnaUpdate ID=62].
9. "Buffy's Religion." *Christianity Today*, July 17, 2002 [http://www. christianitytoday.com/ct/2002/008/36.10.html].
10. With a nod to Elizabeth Kübler Ross.
11. Matthew 19:13–15.
12. Luke 9:54.
13. Acts 13:45, 18:6.
14. 2 Corinthians 2:16.

Chapter Three

1. Quoted in Tiplady, R. "Let X = X: Generation X and World Mission," Apr. 13, 2000 [http://www.postmission.com/articles/letxequalx.pdf]. Tiplady attributes the line to "a now-famous quote in the *Independent* newspaper in 1987."

2. Elbert, P. "Book Reviews." *Asian Journal of Pentecostal Studies*, 2001, 4(2), 332. For an example of this debate among practitioners, see "Great Debate: Is Postmodernism in the Church Overblown?" *Leadership Weekly* (n.d.) [http://www.christianitytoday.com.au/leaders/special/postmodernism.html].

3. Van Gelder, C. "Postmodernism and Evangelicals: A Unique Missiological Challenge at the Beginning of the 21st Century." *Missiology*, Oct. 2002, p. 492.

4. Jean-François Lyotard describes postmodernism as "incredulity toward metanarratives," a rejection of any totalizing account of reality, in his seminal work *The Postmodern Condition: A Report on Knowledge* (Minneapolis: University of Minnesota Press, 1999), p. xxiv; Mouw, R. J. "Pentecostal Evangelism." *Word and World*, 1996, 16(3), 354–357.

5. Hinkson, J., and Ganssle, G. "Epistemology at the Core of Postmodernism: Rorty, Foucault, and the Gospel." In D. A. Carson (ed.), *Telling the Truth: Evangelizing Postmoderns*. Grand Rapids, Mich.: Zondervan, 2000, pp. 68–69. Michel Foucault and Richard Rorty are seminal postmodern thinkers, with Foucault being best known for the concept of power/knowledge and Rorty for his work on pragmatism. See Rorty, R. *Objectivity, Relativism and Truth*. Cambridge: Cambridge University Press, 1991; for commentary on Rorty, see Guignon, C., and Hiley, D. R. (eds.). *Richard Rorty*. Cambridge: Cambridge University Press, 2003; Foucault, M. *Power/Knowledge: Selected Interviews and Other Writings, 1972–1977*. Westminster: Pantheon Books, 1981; for commentary on Foucault, see Bernauer, J., and Carrette, J. (eds.). *Michel Foucault and Theology*. Williston, Vt.: Ashgate, 2003.

6. Weathers, R. A. "Jerry H. Gill's Postmodern Philosophy of Religion: An Evangelical Option?" In D. S. Dockery (ed.), *The Challenge of Postmodernism: An Evangelical Engagement*. Grand Rapids, Mich.: Baker, 1997, p. 104.

7. Grenz, S. J. "Engaging Our Postmodern Culture: An Interview with Stanley Grenz." n.d. [http://www.theooze.com/articles/article.cfm?id=15&page=1].

8. Guinness, O. "Calling, Postmodernism, and Chastened Liberals: A Conversation with Os Guinness." *Mars Hill Review*, Summer 1997, 8, 5–6 [http://www.leaderu.com/marshill/mhr08/os1.html]. A rebuttal to Guinness is found in McLaren's "They Say It's Just a Phase," *Next-Wave*, Apr. 2001 [http://www.next-wave.org/apr01/phase.htm]; accessed May 3, 2001.

9. Morgenthaler, S. "Is Post-Modernism Passé?" *Rev*, Sept./Oct. 2001, p. 69; Erickson, M. J. *Truth or Consequences: The Promise and Perils of Postmodernism*. Downers Grove, Ill.: InterVarsity Press, 2001, p. 320.

10. Smith, C. *Soul Searching: The Religious and Spiritual Lives of American Teenagers*. New York: Oxford University Press, 2005, p. 266.

11. National Aeronautics and Space Administration. "Near Earth Object Program." n.d. [http://neo.jpl.nasa.gov/torino_scale.html].

12. I'm sure I owe at least part of this metaphor to Douglas Coupland's novel *Generation X: Tales for an Accelerated Culture* (New York: St. Martin's Griffin, 1991) in which one of the characters tells the story of an asteroid called Texlahoma—on which it is always 1974.

13. Van Gelder (2002), pp. 492, 495.

14. Van Gelder (2002), pp. 492, 495.

15. Bednar, T. "Why Rick Warren and the Purpose Driven Church Model Will Not Evangelize the 21st Century," June 13, 2005 [http://e-church.com/Blog.asp?EntryID=345 blog 1.14.03].

16. Luke 19:10.

17. Van Rheenen, G. "Evangelizing Folk Religionists." *MMR* (e-mail newsletter) no. 23, Mar. 12, 2002 [http://missiology.org/MMR/

mmr23.html]. I am indebted to Van Rheenen for the connection between postmodernism and folk religion.

18. Ephesians 6:12.
19. 1 Corinthians 4:20.

Chapter Four

1. In an Amazon.com title search for "reverse mentoring," I found one book and one downloadable journal article in May 2006. More than eleven hundred book titles turned up in a search for "mentoring." A Google search in the same month for "reverse mentoring" produced 14,700 hits, while "mentoring" elicited 128,000,000. Google images had 143,000 hits on "mentoring," but only 21 hits on "reverse mentoring" (accessed May 14, 2006). If these numbers have any significance, perhaps they tell us that most people believe there is little future in being a protégé.

2. "The Kids Are All Right." Economist.com, Dec. 21, 2000 [http://www.economist.com/surveys/displayStory.cfm?Story_id =455152]; accessed Sept. 29, 2005.

3. "When Cultures Collide." Economist.com, Dec. 21, 2000 [http://www.economist.com/surveys/displayStory.cfm?Story_id =455224]; accessed Sept. 29, 2005.

4. "Know Future." Economist.com, Dec. 21, 2000 [http://www.economist.com/surveys/displayStory.cfm?Story_id=455168]; accessed Sept. 29, 2005.

5. Adapted from Berger, A. A. "Introduction: Homo Postmodernus: A New Kind of Human Being?" In A. A. Berger (ed.), *The Postmodern Presence: Readings on Postmodernism in American Culture and Society*. Walnut Creek, Calif.: AltaMira Press, 1998.

6. "Tacit Knowledge." Wikipedia, n.d. [http://en.wikipedia.org/wiki/Tacit_knowledge].

7. Joseph, J. "Upward Mentoring: The Wharton Fellows in eBusiness." *Wharton Leadership Digest*, 2001, 5(4) [http://leadership.wharton.upenn.edu/digest/01-01.shtml#Upward%20Mentoring:%20%20The%20Wharton%20Fellows%20in%20eBusiness%20%A0]; accessed Sept. 9, 2005.

8. Alvin Taylor, quoted by S. Pearson and M. Mohan in Coutu, D. "Too Old to Learn?" *Harvard Business Review*, Nov.-Dec. 2000, p. 10.

9. "Know Future" (2000). "Joshua Meyrowitz argues in 'No Sense of Place: The Impact of Electronic Media on Social Behaviour' that baby boomers began to have their 'situational geography' remapped starting with the spread of TV in 1953. When the first TV generation hit eighteen, it set off the 'youth movement' of the late 1960s. Count to eighteen after the start of personal computing with the Apple II in 1977, and you get to the Internet. Marc Andreessen, born in 1971, was one of the first to grow up with the personal computer. In 1995 he took Netscape (the web browser company he cofounded) public, setting off the Internet revolution."

10. Alan Webber, quoted in Starcevich, M. M. "Survey Results: What Is Unique About Reverse Mentoring?" n.d. [http://www.coachingandmentoring.com/reversementoringresults.html]; accessed Sept. 30, 2005.

11. Higgins, M. C. "Too Old to Learn?" *Harvard Business Review*, Nov.-Dec. 2000, p. 7.

12. Proverbs 27:17.

13. 1 Timothy 5:1–2.

14. "Know Future" (2000).

15. Matthew 11:25, 18:3.

16. Starcevich, "Survey Results."

Chapter Five

1. Luke 15:4, 9, 24.

2. Luke 19:10.

3. Barna (2000), p. 82.

4. I am indebted to Byron Klaus, president of the Assemblies of God Theological Seminary for the conceptual genesis of this list as well as much of the wording.

5. Barna's survey found a spike in church attendance for about a month following September 11; however, the increase was identical to the previous year's seasonal findings and soon fell back to normal levels. "How America's Faith Has Changed Since 9-11." Nov. 26, 2001 [http://www.barna.org/FlexPage. aspx?Page=BarnaUpdate&BarnaUpdateID=102].

6. Luke 15:1–2.

7. Colossians 4:5.

8. Easum, B. "Where Do Visions Come From?" (E-mail, EBA Community Leadership Tip of the Month), Sept. 4, 2002.

9. Barclay, W. *On the Gospel of Luke* (rev. ed.). (Daily Bible Study Series.) Philadelphia: Westminster, 1975, p. 178.

10. Norris, K. "The Dick Staub Interview: Kathleen Norris" [http://www.christianitytoday.com/ct/2002/127/21.0.html].

11. Pagitt, D. *Preaching Reimagined: The Role of the Sermon in Communities of Faith.* Grand Rapids, Mich.: Zondervan, 2005.

12. Pagitt (2005).

Chapter Six

1. John 3:30.

2. Colossians 3:3.

3. "Adherents to John's preaching and baptism certainly existed in the middle of the first century and were widespread. Apollos of Alexandria, who ministered at Ephesus, was one of this company. Aquila and Priscilla later instructed him in the ministry of Christ (Acts 18:24–26). When Paul arrived at Ephesus, he found others who held the same belief. Paul himself brought them into a full understanding of the work of Christ (Acts 19:1–7). It is likely that this halfway understanding persisted among John's converts." Tenney, M. C. "John." In F. E. Gaebelein (ed.), *The Expository Bible Commentary*, Vol. 9. Grand Rapids, Mich.: Regency/Zondervan, 1981, p. 52.

4. John 1:20–21.

5. Acts 10:26.

6. Acts 14:18.

7. Matthew 11:1–6.

8. John 10:41.

9. 1 Kings 3:7–8; Exodus 18:17–18.

10. John 3:28.

11. John 3:29.

12. Hammond, J. S., Keeney, R. L., and Raiffa, H. *Smart Choices: A Practical Guide to Making Better Decisions*. New York: Broadway Books, 1998, p. 110.

13. 1 Samuel 16:7; Proverbs 27:1; Romans 8:26; Ecclesiastes 11:6.

14. James 3:2.

15. Lewis, C. S. *The Four Loves*. Orlando: Harcourt Brace, 1960, p. 169.

16. Matthew 5:23–24.

17. Luke 17:4.

18. Proverbs 24:6.

19. Genesis 3:5.

Chapter Seven

1. Behn, R. "Why Measure Performance: Different Purposes Require Different Measures." *Public Administration Review*, 2003, 63(5), 599. Behn cites Tom Peters and Robert Waterman Jr., *In Search of Excellence* (New York: Doubleday, 1982), who in turn cite Mason Haire. If nothing else, this "chain of custody" certainly indicates that the what-gets-measured aphorism has been around for a long time.

2. Hunter, G. "The Church in Post Christian Culture." *Discernment*, 2005, 10(1, 2), 2.

3. Vijay Govindarajan and Chris Trimble (founding director and executive director of the William F. Achtmeyer Center for Global Leadership at the Tuck School of Business at Dartmouth College), "By the Numbers: You Can't Quantify Learning." *Fast Company*, Apr. 26, 2004 [http://www.fastcompany.

com/resources/columnists/vgct/042604.html]; accessed Sept. 9, 2005.

4. See Chadwick, W. *Sheep Stealing: The Church's Hidden Problems with Transfer Growth*. Downers Grove, Ill.: InterVarsity, 2001.

5. Matthew 22:36–40.

6. Kerr, S. "The Folly of Rewarding A While Hoping for B." *Academy of Management Executives*, 1995, 5(1) [http://www.geocities.com/Athens/Forum/1650/rewardinga.html].

7. Barna, G. *State of the Church 2005*. Ventura, Calif.: Barna Group, 2005, pp. 52–53.

8. Jones, L. B. *Jesus CEO: Using Ancient Wisdom for Visionary Leadership*. New York: Hyperion, 1996; Jones, *Jesus, Life Coach: Learn from the Best*. Nashville, Tenn.: Nelson Business, 2004; Jones, *Jesus, Entrepreneur: Using Ancient Wisdom to Launch and Live Your Dream*. New York: Three Rivers Press, 2002.

9. Matthew 6:19–20.

10. John 4:4–26.

11. John 8:1–11.

12. Matthew 6:5.

13. Acts 15:36; Romans 15:24, 28.

14. Mark 6:44; John 6:10; Acts 2:41, 4:4.

15. Romans 14:10.

16. Romans 14:12–13.

17. "An Interview with U2's Bono." atU2, June 28, 2002 [http://www.atu2.com/news/article.src?ID=2364].

18. Matthew 25:32–40.

19. Hull, B. "It's Just Not Working." Adapted from *Leadership Journal*, Summer 2005, ChristianityToday.com [http://www.christianitytoday.com/le/2005/003/6.26.html]; accessed Sept. 19, 2005.

20. Ephesians 5:23.

21. Ephesians 2:20.

22. Romans 8:29.

23. Kaplan, R. S., and Norton, D. "The Balanced Scorecard: Measures That Drive Performance." *Harvard Business Review*, Jan. 1992. See http://www.balancedscorecard.org/.

24. Babbes, G. "Guest Commentary: Ministries Mired in Mediocrity." *Regent Business Review*, n.d., *31*(2) [http://www.regent.edu/acad/schbus/maz/busreview/v1n2/commentary.html].

25. Ogden, G. *Transforming Discipleship: Making Disciples a Few at a Time*. Downers Grove, Ill.: InterVarsity Press, 2003.

26. McNeal, R. *The Present Future: Six Tough Questions for the Church*. San Francisco: Jossey-Bass, 2003, p. 67.

27. Hull (2005).

Chapter Eight

1. 2 Corinthians 5:18, 19.

2. Jude 1:3.

3. Galatians 1:9.

4. Acts 11:1–3.

5. Acts 15:5.

6. Romans 14; 1 Corinthians 8.

7. Finney, C. *Lectures on Revival*. Minneapolis, Minn.: Bethany House, 1989, pp. 164–165.

8. 2 Corinthians 11:4.

9. 1 Corinthians 9:20–21.

10. Acts 15:8, 9.

11. 1 Corinthians 1:23; Galatians 5:11.

12. Galatians 2:7–21.

13. Erickson, M. *The Postmodern World: Discerning the Times and the Spirit of Our Age*. Wheaton, Ill.: Crossway Books, 2002.

14. Mark 1:21–28.

15. I am avoiding the phrase *emerging church* in this discussion to sidestep the stereotypes, assumptions, and controversies that now encumber it. There have been experimental brands of church in every era going by various names, many of which ultimately became new traditional brands.

16. 1 Corinthians 5:1.

17. Pagitt, D. *Preaching Reimagined*. Grand Rapids, Mich.: Zondervan, 2005.

18. Romans 15:7.

19. Easum, B., and Travis, D. *Beyond the Box: Innovative Churches That Work*. Loveland, Colo.: Group, 2003.

20. Webber, R. *The Younger Evangelicals: Facing the Challenges of the New World*. Grand Rapids, Mich.: Baker, 2002.

21. Saey, C. *Faith of My Fathers: Conversations with Three Generations of Pastors About Church, Ministry, and Culture*. Grand Rapids, Mich.: Zondervan, 2005.

22. John 17:23.

23. Romans 15:6.

24. 1 Corinthians 8.

25. Acts 15:15.

26. Romans 14:1.

27. 1 Corinthians 12:14–27.

28. Galatians 6:10.

29. "Focus on 'Worship Wars' Hides the Real Issues Regarding Connection to God." *Barna Update*. n.d. [http://www.barna. org/FlexPage.aspx?Page=BarnaUpdate&BarnaUpdateID=126]; accessed Nov. 19, 2002.

30. Acts 18:10.

Chapter Nine

1. "And the Envelope Please. . . ." [http://www.beliefnet.com/ story/69/story_6925_1.html]; accessed Dec. 1, 2005.

2. Stott, J. *Basic Christian Leadership: Biblical Models of Church, Gospel and Ministry*. Downers Grove, Ill.: InterVarsity Press, 2002, p. 72. Italics added.

3. Grenz, S. J. *A Primer on Postmodernism*. Grand Rapids, Mich.: Eerdmans, 1996, p. xi. Anyone who knew Stan recognizes the modesty of his comment. His life demonstrates the adage that "there is nothing more practical than a good theory."

4. James 1:22–24.

5. George, T. "A Theology to Die for." Feb. 9, 1998 [http://www. ctlibrary.com/ct/1998/february9/8t2049.html].

6. Osborn, R. "The Possibility of Theology Today." *Theology Today*, Jan. 1999, 55, p. 562.

7. George (1998).

8. Hebrews 1:1–3.

9. Hall, D. J. *The End of Christendom and the Future of Christianity*. Harrisburg, Pa.: Trinity Press International, 1995.

10. Livermore, D. "The Youth Ministry Education Debate: Irrelevant Theorists vs. Mindless Practitioners." *Journal of Youth Ministry*, n.d. [http://ayme.gospelcom.net/jym_article.php?article_id=26]; accessed Dec. 22, 2005.

11. Nelson, P. K. "Impractical Christianity." *Christianity Today*, September 2005 [http://www.christianitytoday.com/ct/2005/009/1.80.html]; accessed Sept. 14, 2005.

12. Matthew 7:21–23.

13. Acts 2:12, 4:7, 5:28, 7:1, 9:30–31, 10:33, 11:42, 16:9, 17:8 and 19.

14. Acts 2:12. Perhaps one reason Paul went to the synagogues first when visiting a new city was that he knew the questions asked there.

15. I am indebted to Byron Klaus for introducing me to the field of theological reflection, and stimulating many of the thoughts represented here. The diagram is adapted from Killen, P. O., and DeBeer, J. *The Art of Theological Reflection*. New York: Crossroad, 2004, pp. 88–89.

16. 2 Corinthians 4:7.

17. Kinast, R. L. *Let Ministry Teach: A Guide to Theological Reflection*. Collegeville, Minn.: Liturgical Press, 1996.

18. See my "I Am a Practical Theologian." *Enrichment Journal* [http://www.enrichmentjournal.org/enrichmentjournal/extra/20030827_theologian.cfm].

19. This expression is used by Kevin Miller, editor of Preaching Today.com and editor-at-large of *Leadership Journal*, when asked in an interview with Stephen Shields what the "emergers" (aka emerging church) have to teach the larger evangelical community. One of Miller's four responses is, "You're on the cutting edge of irrelevance to many." Miller is quoted in Shields, S.

"More on Nomo Pomo: An Interview with Kevin Miller." Apr. 2003, no. 48 [http://www.next-wave.org/apr03/millerinterview.html]; accessed Dec. 22, 2005.

20. George (1998), p. x.

Chapter Ten

1. Zacharias, R. "Reaching the Happy Thinking Pagan." Apr. 1, 1995 [http://ctlibrary.com/14809].

2. In fact, one survey finds only a minority (40 percent) of adult unchurched respondents reporting that a worship service would likely be their main point of contact with a congregation. Barna (2000).

3. Swanson, E. "The Engagement Matrix: Enlarging the Heart, Expanding the Kingdom." 2005 [http://www.pursuantgroup.com/leadnet/advance/jul05s1a.htm]; accessed Sept. 13, 2005.

4. Guthrie, S. "The CT Review: Reimaging Missions." *Christianity Online* (ChristianityToday.com), Apr. 23, 2001 [http://ctlibrary.com/6573].

5. Morris, E. "Hope Presbyterian Church." In Swanson, "Engagement Matrix" (2005).

6. Rorty, R. *Wild Orchids and Trotsky: Messages from American Universities* (M. Edmundson, ed.). New York: Penguin, 1993, pp. 41–42.

7. Luke 9:56.

8. Newbigin, L. *The Gospel in a Pluralistic Society.* Grand Rapids, Mich.: Eerdmans, 1989, p. 22.

9. 1 Corinthians 13:1.

10. Hohstadt, T. Post to FaithConnect e-group, June 24, 2002.

11. Romans 5:5.

12. Easum, B. "The Convergence of Spirit and Technology." *Net Results*, Jan. 2002, *23*, 24–25.

13. See Hoover, S., and others. "Faith Online." Pew Internet and American Life Project, Apr. 7, 2004 [http://www.pewinternet.org/pdfs/PIP_Faith_Online_2004.pdf].

14. Oldenburg, R. *The Great Good Place: Cafes, Coffee Shops, Book-stores, Bars, Hair Salons and Other Hangouts at the Heart of the Community* (3rd ed.). New York: Marlowe & Company, 1999.
15. Luke 24:49.
16. Sarah, writing about being stereotyped as a gen Xer, in Webster, D. D. "Seeker-Sensitive, Not Consumer-Oriented." *Discernment*, Spring/Summer 2005, *10*(1, 2), 9.
17. Barna Group. "How America's Faith Has Changed Since September 11" (2001).
18. Barna Group. "Half of All Adults Say Their Faith Helped Them Personally Handle the 9-11 Aftermath." Sept. 3, 2002 [http://www.barna.org/FlexPage.aspx?Page=BarnaUpdate&BarnaUpdateID=120].
19. 1 Peter 2:9.
20. Acts 8:21.
21. Acts 4:29–31.
22. Acts 16:14.
23. 1 Thessalonians 1:4–6.

Chapter Eleven

1. Acts 2:17.
2. 1 Timothy 3:7.
3. Barclay, W. *The Acts of the Apostles* (rev. ed.). (Daily Bible Study Series.) Philadelphia: Westminster Press, 1976, p. 120.
4. Acts 16:3.
5. Bruce, F. F. *The Acts of the Apostles* (2nd ed.). Grand Rapids, Mich.: Eerdmans, 1952, p. 308.
6. Acts 16:3 The Message.
7. Genesis 17:12; John 7:22.
8. Horton, S. *The Book of Acts*. Springfield, Mo.: Gospel Publishing House, 1981, p. 190.
9. 1 Corinthians 7:19.
10. Galatians 5:6; see also Galatians 6:15.
11. Fernando, A. "Acts." In T. Muck (ed.), *The NIV Application Commentary*. Grand Rapids, Mich.: Zondervan, 1998, p. 436.

12. 1 Corinthians 9:12b.
13. Galatians 5:11.
14. Galatians 5:11.
15. 1 Timothy 1:14.
16. Bruce, F. F. "The Acts of the Apostles." In D. Guthrie and others (eds.), *The New Bible Commentary* (rev. ed.). Grand Rapids, Mich.: Eerdmans, 1970, p. 993.
17. Stott, J.R.W. *The Spirit, the Church, and the World.* Downers Grove, Ill.: InterVarsity Press, 1990, p. 254.
18. "Young Leaders Summit Report." Lifeway, n.d. [http://www.lifeway.com/lwc/article_main_page/0%2C1703%2CA%253D1 60275%2526M%253D150032%2C00.html]; accessed June 2, 2005.
19. C. Strang and L. Rabe, quoted in J. Leland (New York Times News Service), "Young People Turn Against Their Parents' 'Church Lite.' " *Lexington Herald Leader*, posted May 16, 2004 [http://www.kentucky.com/mld/heraldleader/news/nation/8678 837.htm?template=contentM]; accessed May 19, 2004.
20. Fernando (1998), p. 439.
21. Stott (1990), p. 254.
22. Acts 16:9.

Chapter Twelve

1. For more examples, see http://www.oldvan.com/songs/index.htm.
2. "Baby Boomers: From the Age of Aquarius to the Age of Responsibility." Pew Research Center, Dec. 8, 2005 [http://pewresearch.org/reports/?ReportID=2].
3. Easum, B. "It's Time for the Cow to Eat the Cabbage: Christianity Is in Big Trouble in the U.S." (n.d.; author's copy).
4. Acts 16:1–4.
5. Scripture references for Timothy's relationship with Paul include his serving as an extension of Paul's work in Macedonia (Acts 18:5, 19:22); accompanying him in his travels (Acts 20:4; 2 Cor. 1:1); and serving as his emissary to Corinth, Philippi, and Thessalonica (1 Cor. 4:17; Phil. 2:19; 1 Thess.

3:2, 6). Paul described him to the Corinthians as "carrying on the work of the Lord just as I am" (1 Cor. 16:10). Timothy preached Christ in Corinth (2 Cor. 1:19); was mentioned in the introduction to six of Paul's epistles, often as "our brother" (2 Cor. 1:1; Phil. 1:1; Col. 1:1; 1 Thess. 1:1; 2 Thess. 1:1; Philem. 1:1); was described to the Romans as "my fellow worker" (Rom. 16:21); and was imprisoned and released for the gospel's sake (Heb. 13:23).

6. 2 Timothy 4:7.

7. 2 Timothy 4:9.

8. 2 Timothy 1:2.

9. In Titus 1:4 Paul refers to Titus in the same way, as "my true son in our common faith."

10. Barna, G. "Gracefully Passing the Baton." *Barna Update*, Apr. 26, 2004 [http://www.barna.org/FlexPage.aspx?Page=Perspective &PerspectiveID=1].

11. 2 Timothy 1:3–4.

12. Philippians 2:20, 22.

13. Philippians 1:1.

14. 1 Corinthians 4:15.

15. 2 Timothy 1:5.

16. 2 Timothy 1:5.

17. 2 Timothy 3:15.

18. 2 Timothy 1:1.

19. 2 Timothy 1:6–7.

20. 1 Timothy 1:18.

21. 2 Timothy 1:7.

22. McGee, G. B. *People of the Spirit*. Springfield, Mo.: Gospel Publishing House, 2005, p. 116.

23. 1 Timothy 4:12.

24. Hebrews 12:1.

25. 2 Timothy 1:8.

26. Philippians 3:14.

Acknowledgments

All writing is a team sport, so I have many people to thank for making this volume possible and for making me look better than I am. Most of all, I need to thank God for the sacred accidents that connected me with Sheryl Fullerton at Jossey-Bass, Greg Ligon and friends at Leadership Network, and Don Pape at Alive Communication. It all started at a talk I gave in California that went so badly almost half the audience left before the end. But Sheryl stayed, and that started everything. Working with the Jossey-Bass, Leadership Network, and Alive Communication teams has been a pleasure the whole way.

I also owe a great debt to my seminary's administration and faculty, who supported this project with a lot of encouragement and countless hours of dialogue, and by looking the other way when I needed to disappear to work on it. The Doctor of Ministry Team—Cheryl, Lori, Steven, and Tracy—constantly bolstered my spirits, listened to my ventilations by the hour, and covered my absences. God bless them.

My wife Janet stood with me during every minute of this project. I love her for that and for everything else. She knows better than anyone the degree to which *Off-Road Disciplines* grew out of our own struggles.

I dedicate this book also to my father and mother, people of the Spirit. Dad's passing reminded me that leaders and leadership are both finite. Mom's dawn prayers did the rest.

In the end, this volume is like an RSS feed on a web browser (if you don't know what that is, get a Reverse Mentor right away), aggregating the stories of many friends across the country. I thank them all. Their lives really wrote this book; I only composed the words.

The Author

Earl Creps has spent several years on the road studying nontraditional congregations. He brings to this research a background as a pastor, having led three churches (one boomer, one builder, and one gen X); a consultant, having served as his denomination's national adult ministries consultant; and an educator, teaching on mission in emerging culture for the Assemblies of God Theological Seminary (AGTS). He earned a Ph.D. in communication (Northwestern University) and a doctor of ministry degree (AGTS). Currently, he directs the Doctor of Ministry program at AGTS in Springfield, Missouri, and serves as associate professor of leadership and spiritual renewal. He is the author of numerous articles and adult study courses, a speaker for seminars and conferences, and a consultant to both church and parachurch organizations. He and his wife, Janet, live outside Springfield, Missouri.

Index

Other Leadership Network Books of Interest

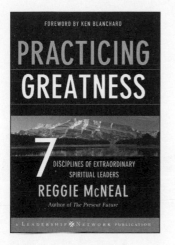

Practicing Greatness
7 Disciplines of Extraordinary Spiritual Leaders
REGGIE MCNEAL
Foreword by Ken Blanchard
Cloth
ISBN: 0–7879–7753–5

"Practicing Greatness is a hard-hitting leadership book, not just a collection of inspirational thoughts."

—from the Foreword by Ken Blanchard, author of *The One-Minute Manager* and *Lead Like Jesus: Lessons from the Greatest Leadership Role Model of All Time*

"The depth and breadth of wisdom in this book is just short of unbelievable. Good leaders aspiring to be great leaders will do well to read this book and allow it to probe and shape their lives."

—Bill Easum, Easum, Bandy & Associates

Based on his experience coaching and mentoring thousands of Christian leaders across a wide variety of settings, best-selling leadership expert and consultant Reggie McNeal shows spiritual leaders how to move from being simply good enough to being great by living seven essential disciplines: self-awareness, management of emotions and expectations, a lifelong commitment to learning, a sense of mission, the ability to make great decisions, the commitment to be in community, and the intentional practice of solitude and contemplation.

REGGIE MCNEAL is the director of leadership development for the South Carolina Baptist Convention. Through his various leadership roles—from local congregational settings to denominational positions, seminary classrooms, and coach and consultant for thousands of spiritual leaders—he has been devoted to helping leaders understand and practice true leadership greatness. McNeal is the author of *Revolution in Leadership: Training Apostles for Tomorrow's Church* (Abingdon Press), along with *A Work of Heart: Understanding How God Shapes Spiritual Leaders* and the best-selling *The Present Future: Six Tough Questions for the Church*, both from Jossey-Bass.

Other Leadership Network Books of Interest

The Present Future
Six Tough Questions for the Church
REGGIE MCNEAL
Cloth
ISBN: 0–7879–6568–5

"This is the most courageous book I have ever read on church life. McNeal nails the problem on the head. Be prepared to be turned upside down and shaken loose of all your old notions of what church is and should be in today's world."

—George Cladis, senior pastor,
Westminster Presbyterian Church, Oklahoma City;
author, *Leading the Team-Based Church*

"With humor and rare honesty Reggie McNeal challenges church leaders to take authentic Christianity back into the real world. He's asking the right questions to help us get back on track."

—Tommy Coomes, contemporary Christian music pioneer and
record producer, artist with Franklin Graham Ministries

"Reggie McNeal throws a lifeline to church leaders who are struggling with consumer-oriented congregations wanting church for themselves. The Present Future will recharge your passion."

—Rev. Robert R. Cushman, senior pastor,
Princeton Alliance Church, Plainsboro, New Jersey

In this provocative book, author, consultant, and church leadership developer Reggie McNeal identifies the six most important realities that church leaders must address including: recapturing the spirit of Christianity and replacing "church growth" with a wider vision of kingdom growth; developing disciples instead of church members; fostering the rise of a new apostolic leadership; focusing on spiritual formation rather than church programs; and shifting from prediction and planning to preparation for the challenges of an uncertain world. McNeal contends that by changing the questions church leaders ask themselves about their congregations and their plans, they can frame the core issues and approach the future with new eyes, new purpose, and new ideas.

REGGIE MCNEAL is the director of leadership development for the South Carolina Baptist Convention. Through his various leadership roles—from local congregational settings to denominational positions, seminary classrooms, and coach and consultant for thousands of spiritual leaders—he has been devoted to helping leaders understand and practice true leadership greatness. McNeal is the author of *Revolution in Leadership: Training Apostles for Tomorrow's Church* (Abingdon Press), along with *A Work of Heart: Understanding How God Shapes Spiritual Leaders* and *Practicing Greatness: 7 Disciplines of Extraordinary Spiritual Leaders*, both from Jossey-Bass.

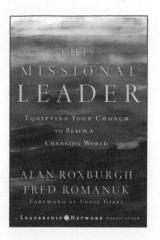

The Missional Leader

Equipping Your Church to Reach a Changing World

ALAN ROXBURGH and FRED ROMANUK

Foreword by Eddie Gibbs

Cloth

ISBN: 0–7879–8325-X

"Discontinuous change wreaks havoc among congregations and pastors who aren't familiar with the new terrain. When it comes to navigating this new land, Roxburgh and Romanuk have my ear and gratitude. Effective, dependable, useful . . . their wisdom is helping retool our congregation for daring and robust witness. And among my students—who feel change deep in their bones, both its threats and opportunities—this book is a vital companion as they begin their ministries."

—Chris William Erdman, senior pastor, University Presbyterian Church; adjunct faculty, MB Biblical Seminary Biblical Seminary

In *The Missional Leader,* consultants Alan Roxburgh and Fred Romanuk give church and denominational leaders, pastors, and clergy a clear model for leading the change necessary to create and foster a missional church focused outward to spread the message of the Gospel into the surrounding community. *The Missional Leader* emphasizes principles rather than institutional forms, shows readers how to move away from "church as usual," and demonstrates what capacities, environments, and mindsets are required to lead a missional church.

Experts in the field of missional leadership, Roxburgh and Romanuk outline a strategic change model that can be implemented to help transform a congregation and its leaders. They also present the factors that define the character of an effective missional leader and show how a pastor and other clergy can lead their congregation to best serve their church and larger community.

ALAN ROXBURGH is a pastor, teacher, writer, and consultant with more than thirty years' experience in church leadership, consulting, and seminary education. He works with the Allelon Missional Leadership Network in the formation of leaders for the missional church.

FRED ROMANUK is an organizational psychologist who has led strategic planning initiatives for many large organizations in Canada and the United States. He has also worked with senior executives in assessing and developing the capabilities of people in leadership roles.

Other Leadership Network Books of Interest

Organic Church
Growing Faith Where Life Happens
NEIL COLE
Foreword by Leonard I. Sweet
Cloth
ISBN: 0–7879–8129-X

"This book is profound, practical, and a pleasure to read. It stretches our thinking and brings us to a place where we can see the Kingdom of God spread across the world in our generation. This book has come at the right time."

—John C. Maxwell, founder, INJOY,
INJOY Stewardship Services and EQUIP

"My life is about seeing hundredfold results. Neil Cole's approach helps get those kinds of results for churches by planting many new expressions of the Kingdom that reach thousands of people. One of the great joys of my life for the past six years has been to watch the dramatic growth of Awakening Chapels and the organic churches described in this work. Cole's new book tells not only the inspiring story but also describes the principles, so you can apply these ideas."

—Bob Buford, founder and chairman, Leadership Network;
author, Halftime and Finishing Well

For many young people, traditional models of church hold very little appeal. They see themselves as more spiritual than religious and are looking for deeper, more authentic relationships with other people and with God. Church leaders and planners are realizing that they must go to where these people already are—in coffeehouses, bars, pubs, and other "third places"—if they want to connect with them and eventually interest these young people in Christianity. *Organic Church* offers a guide for demystifying this new model of church and shows how to undertake the practical aspects of implementing it. Instead of bringing people into a traditional church, this model helps bring faith to where life happens.

NEIL COLE is a church starter and pastor, and founder and executive director of Church Multiplication Associates, which has helped start over seven hundred churches in thirty-two states and twenty-three nations in six years. He is an international speaker and the author of *Cultivating a Life for God*.